THE CELL BLOCK PRESENTS...

THE CEO MANUAL

Published by: THE CELL BLOCK™

THE CELL BLOCK
P.O. Box 1025
Rancho Cordova, CA 95741

Website: thecellblock.net
Facebook/thecellblockofficial
Instagram: @mikeenemigo
Corrlinks: info@thecellblock.net

Cover design by Mike Enemigo

Send comments, reviews, or other business inquiries:
Visit our website: info@thecellblock.net

Note: This book is also published as *CEO MANUAL: START
A BUSINESS, BE A BOSS*

CONTENTS

5 CORE STEPS TO STARTING YOUR OWN BUSINESS

1. START IT

Business startup isn't rocket science; it's not as complicated or scary as people think. Once you have a great idea, product or service in mind, it's a step-by-step common-sense process. Here's step one: Figure out what you want to do and *do* it.

2. PLAN IT

If you build it, will they buy it? Determining whether there really is a market for your product or service is fundamental. Consider market research an investment in your future product or service. Make the necessary adjustments now that will save you money in the long run.

3. FUND IT!

Figure out where the money will come from. The best place to begin is by looking in the mirror. Self-financing is the number-one source of income for startup – and it creates faith in your company when you need more cash. Get the expert advice on how to approach bankers, investors, or crowdfund.

4. MARKET IT!

It's essential that you spread the word about your company/product/service. You can create a brand identity and develop a marketing campaign that works without spending a fortune. However, an investment of your time is required.

5. PROFIT FROM IT!

Make sure you're in love with the profit, *not* the product. Many people get emotional about their business, which clouds their judgment. Keeping score with basic bookkeeping and financial statements will help you effectively manage your finances and keep the profits coming.

YOU MUST READ THIS TO IMPROVE YOUR CHANCES AT BUSINESS SUCCESS!

The number of new business failures continues unabated. Here are the most common causes of failure you must avoid in order to improve your chances of success...

Lack of a Business Plan

You would think that anyone contemplating starting a business, considering the amount of time, effort and money involved, would develop a business plan, right? WRONG! The majority of new businesses are launched by entrepreneurs without a plan! Consequently, entrepreneurs get into trouble because they haven't considered all of the aspects associated with starting and managing a successful business.

Why is that? The typical entrepreneur (and his collegues with whom he starts) is a "techie" of one type of another. I affectionately call them business innocents – the founder and his soul brothers.

Many times techies have never taken any courses on business (e.g. management, accounting, marketing, or planning). They are unaware of the fundamentals of what is required to run a business. And as a result, they experience a predictable series of natural pitfalls.

Insufficient Cash

Without a budget or even a break-even analysis, entrepreneurs rapidly squander their precious cash and waste valuable time. Entrepreneurs are long on ideas, but notoriously short on cash.

Entrepreneurs are very optimistic and perceive that everything will happen faster than is possible. In life – as in business – results usually take longer and costs more than expected.

Looking at their business with short-sighted time horizons, entrepreneurs expect to open their doors and become swamped with paying customers that will generate short-term cash and sustain the early stages of the business.

Unfortunately, even under the best circumstances, the typical start-up requires 18 to 24 months to generate positive cash flow. The statistics are well-known, and on average, 95% of all new businesses fail in the initial years of their existence.

You would also think that these well-published statistics would prompt entrepreneurs to plan better and have sufficient cash to fund their start-ups for at least the first year or more, right?

No Accounting Skills

Business is about numbers – sales, costs, expenses, profits – quantifiable transactions. If Wal-Mart knows what they sell in every store around the world, isn't that a strong indication of how critical it is to account for every aspect of your new business?

You can't manage what you don't know. Since entrepreneur's dislike controls, have no budgets, and typically haven't done a break-even analysis, is it any surprise that so many new businesses fail? The simple fact is that it costs a certain amount of money to start almost any kind of business.

4

So the new business owner must calculate how much they must sell just to cover all costs and expenses they will inevitably incur, and by what date they must have them covered.

How many meals in the restaurant? How many bagels in the bagel shop? How many cupcakes in a Mr. Cupcakes? How many pizzas in a pizza parlor?

Everything about running a business is about numbers – cash flow. If you don't keep track of every dollar spent and every dollar made in a timely fashion, then there can only be one result. Trouble!

Since CASH is KING, every penny needs to be accounted for in a proper fashion. Once you start your business, the money clocks start ticking. If you spend more than you generate, there can only be one outcome – failure!

Lack of accounting controls, budgets and timely reporting of results is one of the major problems start-up businesses experiences. Surprises can be deadly!

Selling vs. Marketing

Entrepreneurs are great salesmen. They are selling their idea for a better world. Unfortunately, they overestimate the number of customers that will find their solution applicable to them. Or they misinterpret the perceived worth of their value proposition. They also frequently misjudge how fast customers will adopt their solution. In addition, there are only so many hours to make sales in every day. Eventually, the typical entrepreneur runs out of time, energy, and resources.

Somewhere along the way, the typical entrepreneur has to realize that there are just not enough hours to sell, and they must transition their efforts from selling to marketing. Selling is asking for the order. Marketing is creating a demand in the mind of the customer so that they seek you out.

Poor People Skills

Management is simply getting things done through people. Entrepreneurs tend to be one man/woman shows. Running a successful business is a team effort.

The most successful firms constantly tout their people. They believe in every member of the team working together to deliver great products with excellent customer service.

The inability of the owner/founder to delegate authority and responsibility is another contributing factor to early demise of their business. Typical start-ups are helter skelter operations with everybody doing everything – including the founder. If allowed to continue, the only result can be chaos, confusion and the waste of precious resources.

When crisis management is the order of the day, failure isn't too far away. So with no plan, insufficient cash, poor accounting controls, no organizational structure and a sell everything-to-everybody modus of operandi, what can the result be?

Remember: Nobody plans to fail...they just fail to plan.

A business plan is a relatively inexpensive exercise done on paper before you can start your business. It can save you from yourself!

5 COMMON LAUNCH ERRORS YOU MUST AVOID!

1. Insistence on autonomy

In the startup phase, the company is all about you. Your fingerprints are on everything, and there is very little you don't know and aren't directing. But after the startup phase, the company streams into the growth phase, becoming more complex and more vulnerable to industry and economic trends. At that point, an entrepreneur's insistence on autonomy can hinder the company's ability to respond quickly and intelligently to challenges it faces.

2. Unwillingness to build structure

Many entrepreneurs will need to surround themselves with a strong executive team – or at least a steady right-hand individual – to ensure the company's success. But too many business owners fail to create the kind of structure that produces good leadership decisions within a managerial team. The entrepreneur needs to know the employees and where their strengths lie to put them to good use.

3. Lack of financial leadership

Entrepreneurs by definition take risk when they make the decision to start their own business. In the area of financial leadership, which includes tracking cash levels and trends, financial covenants, metrics and expenses, entrepreneurs who are not financially literate and active will need the direct support of a financial expert to ensure they receive the advice and input needed in their organization.

4. Reacting unwisely to boredom

Starting a business proved exhilarating. The day-to-day operation of it may pale in comparison. A bored entrepreneur can create significant troubles for the business. Things will get up-ended in a hurry, because many bored entrepreneurs either start new companies or abruptly make changes in their current company to keep their own level of excitement high.

5. Failure to engage in self-examination

Entrepreneurs need to be aware of their own strengths and weaknesses, the same things they engage in their employees.

NAMING YOUR BUSINESS

If you're anything like me, you've already got the perfect name for your business, plus ten other names you had to choose between. After all, most of us have a dream of starting our own company long before we actually have the ability to do so, and creating the perfect name is often our first step. However, in the event you have not thought of the perfect name just yet (or even if you have), here are five tips to assist you in making the perfect decision.

1. Think marketing:

First, decide on the advertising that will drive 90 percent of your business. Will you rely primarily on print ads, word-of-mouth, the internet, Yellow Pages, radio or some combination thereof? Depending on your answers to these questions, certain criteria become very important. Overdone literation, foreign words and domain names with hyphens are the kiss of death for websites and radio ads, where spelling and easy pronunciation are critical. If your business will be driven by a Directory, like the Yellow Pages, an old trick is picking a company name that starts with A, B, or C so your ad will be placed toward the front if it's section. A lot of people search using the internet, so having a name that people might google when searching for your type of business or product could be very beneficial.

2. Scan the competition:

Compiling the names of competitors offers a starting point for differentiating yourself. Do your competitors' names really fit the target market? Are the names too plain and traditional while the customer is cool and swaggy? The answers will tell you what doesn't work, which can help you narrow your list of possibilities.

3. Get brainstorming:

Do a brain dump of every possibility that comes to mind, including ideas you get from companies outside your industry. Think of buzzwords that appeal to your potential customer and that the competition isn't using, and consider the result the customer wants from using your product or service. You want something that will stand out. "Hood Millionaire" tells you exactly what we have and what we're about, just from those two words.

4. Check for negative connotations.

Names like Cobweb Design, Goose chase and Wild Weasel, may sound clever, but they can leave potential customers with an unsettled feeling about your product or service before they even try it. There's one company called Hustle University, which I think is dope, but sometimes I've seen it shortened to "Hustle U". See what I'm saying? Consider every word on your list for negative meanings, and ask friends and family how different words strike them. Scratch potential offenders off your list. Think about where you want to go with your business, too. It may be a good idea to have the name of your city or hood in your company name if your only plan on the business being in your city or hood, but it may not work well if you plan on eventually growing to another city, state, or even country. Think ahead.

5. Check for trademarks.

More than one business owner has come up with a company name and put it out there, only to receive a cease-and-desist order that forces him or her back to the drawing board. If you learn this too late, after you've printed material, advertised, etc., it can be a very costly mistake. So, before you commit yourself in any way to commissioning a logo, putting up a website, making signage, products and so on, make sure the name is legally available. You can search for registered trademarks at www.uspto.gov. Later I'll show you how to trademark your own name.

The name game is important, so take it seriously. It has the potential to help, or hurt. And if you're a savvy hustler, you'll pick a name that a movement can be built upon like Hood Millionaire. I currently create and sell self-help info that teaches the urban community how to hustle and win legally, but which one of you wouldn't rock a shirt, hat or medallion, that says Hood Millionaire? Pick a name that can be a business in and of itself.... Can ya dig it?

THE MISSION STATEMENT

Mission Statement: a short official statement than an organization makes about the work that it does and why it does it.

The "mission statement" is a system that Napoleon Bonaparte initiated and it has been imitated by the greatest generals of the modern era. Napoleon would give his field marshals a clear sense of the goals for a particular campaign or battle – what has become known as the "mission statement" – and they were then empowered to reach those on their own, in their own way. All that mattered were the results. The idea behind it is that those who are fighting on the ground often have a better sense of what needs to be done in the here and now; they have more information at their fingertips than the leader. With a degree of trust in their decisions, they can operate fast and feel more engaged in the execution of the war. This revolutionary system allowed Napoleon's army to move with greater speed and to cultivate a team of highly experienced and brilliant field marshals. And it took great courage to trust in them and not try to control everything on the battlefield.

As the CEO of your company, you are the general. It is your job to come up with your company's mission statement (every company has one) so that your team has a clear idea regarding what your company's concepts and objectives are.

Here's an example of one company's mission statement, and perhaps the most genius use of one I've ever seen:

"This is your life. Do what you love, and do it often. If you don't like something, change it. If you don't like your job, quit. If you don't have enough time, stop watching TV. If you are looking for the love of your life, stop; they will be waiting for you when you start doing things you love. Stop over analyzing, life is simple. All emotions are beautiful. When you eat, appreciate every last bite. Open your mind, arms, and heart to new things and people, we are united in our differences. Ask the next person you see what their passion is, and share your inspiring dream with them. Travel often; getting lost will help you find yourself. Some opportunities only come once, seize them. Life is about the people you meet, and the things you create with them, so go out and start creating. Life is short. Live your dream and share your passion."

Most mission statements contain words like value and service but often fail to explain what the founders truly care about, much less inspire anyone else to care. Holstee's mission statement is an exception. The Brooklyn, New York-based Company which sells eco-friendly clothing and accessories, rose from obscurity after its statement, dubbed the Holstee manifesto, and went viral. The document has been viewed online more than 50 million times and translated into 12 languages. When Holstee turned the message into a $25 poster – printed on recycled paper, of course – the item quickly became one of the company's top sellers. Holstee's co-founders, Fabian Pfortmuller and Brothers Mike and Dave Radparvar, were as surprised as anyone that their mission statement, once tucked away on the About Us page of Holstee's website, resonated so strongly with so many people. Here is a quick interview with Pfortmuller about the impact a strong mission statement can have on a company.

How did you come up with your mission statement?

We wrote it a few months after we started Holstee, in 2009. We were talking about how every entrepreneur, including us, wants to build a lifestyle for himself. But even though you're your own boss, sometimes a start-up becomes something you can't control. You build your business, but at the end of the day, you might not even want to work there. So we wanted to define what success means to us in nonmonetary terms.

We also knew that down the road, it would help to have a reminder of why we started Holstee. Dave and Mike quit their jobs in the middle of a recession to start the company. The manifesto was a reminder that we took all these risks for a reason, to live a lifestyle we loved.

How did it get so big?

Two bloggers picked it up. That just kicked off a chain reaction. We saw it all over Tumblr and Twitter. People started making it their Facebook photo. We were so surprised at how people responded to it. I think society is just hungry for genuine values.

Who's idea was it to turn the manifesto into merchandise?

Actually, customers started asking for it. At first, we were hesitant about putting it on a poster. It was really personal to us, and putting anything on a big poster or T-shirt can cheapen it. But we got so many requests that one of our freelancers convinced us to try it. We got amazing feedback. We sold about 11,000 posters last year [$25 x 11,000 = $275,000!]. They accounted for roughly 50 percent of our revenue in November.

How has the popularity of the posters influenced your brand?

Usually people make a product first, then build a brand around it. In our case, it happened the other way around. That has helped us build trust with our customers. People see the manifesto and automatically understand what we stand for. Then again, we're not a manifesto company, whatever that would be. The success of the posters helped us bootstrap, but at the end of the day, we're about products with a unique story that are designed with a conscience.

There are a lot of great lines in there. What's your favorite?

Life is about the people you meet and the things you create with them." I strongly believe that. Here at Holstee, I have the luck of working with my two best friends. We live together. We work together. We really live that.

Do you have any advice for business owners who want to create an inspiring mission statement?

Write it for yourself. Mission statements of large organizations sound meaningless, because they're written to convince an audience. It's going to work only if it's genuine. We had selfish reasons for creating Holstee. We wanted to create great products, but we also wanted to have fun doing it. For us, it was more genuine to write about a lifestyle. If we can do all those things we mentioned, like travel, eat well, and build strong relationships, we'll be happier and build a better company because of it.

Note from Mike: This story inspired me and gave me a new perspective about ways to build a lifestyle brand. In my opinion, their story/experience is the essence of that. Via T-shirts and greeting cards, they're making a very nice income off their mission statement alone. Brilliant.

TRADEMARK, COPYRIGHT, OR PATENT?

A trademark is generally a word, phrase, symbol, or design, or a combination thereof, that identifies and distinguishes the source of the goods of one party from those of others.

- A service mark is the same as a trademark, except it identifies and distinguishes the source of a service rather than goods.

Do trademarks, copyrights, and patents protect the same things?

No. Trademarks, copyrights and patents protect different types of intellectual property.

A trademark typically protects brand names and logos used on goods and services. A copyright protects an original artistic or literary work. A patent protects an invention. For example, if you invent a new kind of vacuum cleaner, you would apply for a patent to protect the invention itself. You would apply to register a trademark to protect the brand name of the vacuum cleaner. And you might register a copyright for the TV commercial that you use to market the product.

For copyright information, go to www.copyright.gov. for patent information, go to www.uspto.gov/patents.

You help evaluate your overall awareness of intellectual property knowledge and to provide access to additional educational materials based on the assessment rules, you can use the Intellectual Property Awareness Assessment tool, available at http://www.uspto.gov/inventors/assessment/.

How do domain names, business name registrations, and trademarks differ?

A domain name is part of a web address that links to the internet protocol address (IP address) of a particular website. For example, in the web address "www.uspto.gov," the domain name is "uspto.gov." The domain name for The Cell Block is thecellblock.net. You register your domain name with an accredited domain name registrar, not through the USPTO. A domain name and a trademark differ. A trademark identifies goods or services being from a particular source. Use of a domain nam1 only as part of a web address does not qualify as source indicating trademark us, though other prominent us apart from the web address may qualify as trademark use. Registration of a domain name with a domain name registrar does not give you any trademark rights. For example, even if you register a certain domain name with a domain name registrar, you could later be required to surrender it if it infringes on someone else's trademark rights.

Similarly, use of a business name does not necessarily qualify as trademark use, though other use of a business name all the source of goods or services may qualify it as both a business name and a trademark. Many states and local jurisdictions register business names, either as part of obtaining a certificate to do business or as an assumed name filing. For example, in a state where you will be doing business, you might file documents (typically with a state corporation commission or state division of corporations) to form a business entity, such as a corporation or limited liability company. You would select a name for your entity; for example, Hood Millionaire, LLC. If no other company has already applied for the exact name in that state and you comply with all other requirements, the state would likely issue you a certificate and authorize you to do business under that name. However, a state's authorization to form a business with a particular name does not also give you trademark rights and other parties could later try to prevent your use of the business name if they believe a likelihood of confusion exists with their trademarks.

For more information on trademarks, visit www.uspto.gov/trademarks. For assistance visit trademarkassistancecenter@uspto.gov. You can also write and request a free "Basic Facts About Trademarks" booklet from Commissioner for Trademarks; PO Box 1451; Alexandria, VA 22313-1451.

WRITING A BUSINESS PLAN

After you've thought about what type of business you want, the next step is to develop a business plan. Think of a business plan as the roadmap with milestones for the business. It begins as a reassessment tool to determine profitability and market share, and then expand as an in-business assessment tool to determine success, obtain financing and determine repayment ability, among other factors. Creating a comprehensive business plan can be a long process, and you need good advice. The SBA and its resource partners, including Small Business Development Centers, have the expertise to help you craft a winning business plan. The SBA also offers online (www.sba.gov) templates to get you started.

In general, however, just to give you an overview, a good business plan contains:

Introduction...

- Give a detailed description of the business and its goals.

- Discuss ownership of the business and its legal structure.

- List the experience and skills you bring to the business.

- Discuss the advantages you and your business have over competitors.

Marketing...

- Discuss the products and services your company will offer.

- Identify customer demand for your products and services.

- Identify your market, its size and locations.

- Explain how your products and services will be advertised and marketed.

- Explain your pricing strategy.

Financial Management...

- Develop an expected return on investment and monthly cash flow for the first year.

- Provide projected income statements and balance sheets for a two-year period.

- Discuss your break-even point.

- Explain your personal balance sheet and method of compensation.

- Discuss who will maintain your accounting records and how they will be kept.

- Provide "what if" statements addressing alternative approaches to potential problems.

Operations...

- Explain how the business will be managed day-to-day.

- Discuss hiring and personal procedures.

- Discuss insurance, lease or rent agreements.

- Account for the equipment necessary to produce your goods or services.

- Account for production and delivery of products and services.

Concluding Statement...

Summarize your business goals and objectives and express your commitment to the success of your business. Once you have completed your business plan, review it with a friend or business associate and a professional business counselor. And remember, the business plan is a flexible document that should change as your business grows.

CEO SECRET TO AN INSTANT BUSINESS PLAN!

When applying for a bank loan, it will want to see a business plan. Instead of writing one yourself, use this smart trick. Ask the bank officer to tell you in detail what the ideal plan would look like. Ask how many pages, types of charts and graphs, even ask him what color paper. Then ask him to show you an old plan that he approved (with the name blacked out). Now all you have to do is make your plan exactly the same as the plan the bank showed you. Bam! You have an instant plan, and it's sure to be approved because you're giving them exactly what they want.

BUSINESS ORGANIZATION: CHOOSING YOUR BUSINESS STRUCTURE

There are many forms of legal structure you may choose for your business. Each legal structure offers organizational options with different tax a liability issue. I suggest you research each legal structure thoroughly and consult a tax accountant and/or attorney prior to making your decision. The most common organizational structures are sole proprietorships, general and limited partnerships and limited liability companies. Each structure offers unique tax and liability benefits. If you're uncertain which business format is right for you, you may want to discuss options with a business counselor or attorney. However, here is a brief overview.

Sole Proprietorship...

One person operating a business as an individual is a sole proprietorship. It's the most common form of business organization. Profits are taxed as income to the owner personally. The personal tax rate is usually lower than the corporate tax rate. The owner has complete control of the business, but faces unlimited liability for its debts. There is very little government regulation or reporting required with this business structure.

General Partnership...

A partnership exists when two or more persons join together in the operation and management of a business. Partnerships are subject to relatively little regulation and are fairly easy to establish. A formal partnership agreement is recommended to address potential conflicts such as: who will be responsible for performing each task; what, if any, consultation is needed between partners before major decisions, and what happens if/when a partner dies. Under a general partnership each partner is liable for all debts of the business. Profits are taxed as income to the partners based on their ownership percentage.

Limited Partnership...

Like a general partnership, a limited partnership is established by an agreement between two or more persons. However, there are two types of partners.

- A general partner has greater control in some aspects of the partnership. For example, only a general partner can decide to dissolve the partnership. General partners have no limits on the dividends they can receive from profit so they can incur unlimited liability.

- Limited partners can only receive a share of profits based on the proportional amount of their investment, and liability is similarly limited in proportion to their investment.

LLCs and LLPs...

The Limited Liability Company or partnership is a relatively new business form. It combines selected corporate and partnership characteristics while still maintaining status as a legal entity distinct from its owners. As a separate entity it can acquire assets, incur liabilities and conduct business. It limits liability for the owners. The limited liability partnership is similar to the LLC, but it is for professional organizations.

While those may be the most popular structures, there is something else you should consider if it can at all apply to you and what you're doing. What is it?

Non-Profit Organization...

One of the biggest misconceptions is that people who organize and run not-for-profit corporations don't take out much for themselves. The truth is that fundraisers and top officers of outfits like Red Cross are extremely well paid. Worthy activities that non-profit groups can include, but are not limited to, are any educational, medical, scientific, religious, or pretty much any do-gooder activity you can think of. For example, I can start Hood Millionaire University, where I educate underprivileged teens in the urban community how to hustle and win legally. Can ya dig it?

People who raise money for such enterprises typically get commissions of up to half of what they collect. The amounts can be substantial. An outfit called "Glide" gives away food to poor kids. In 2010 they raised close to $3,000,000.00 at one crack by auctioning off "Lunch with the Third Richest Man in the World, Warren Buffet." I don't think anyone got a 50 percent commission, but you can be sure the people running the charity did very well. The government typically allows non-profit groups to incorporate for free. The IRS allows donors to reduce their taxes by giving to these non-profits. Radio and TV stations in the US and many other countries are required by law to give time and space to promoting their activities. The United Nations gives many Non-Government Organizations "Observer Status." The ability to mingle with and influence UN representatives has a definite monetary value. Governments and international organizations routinely give NGOs serious grants running into the millions. If you pay taxes, a lot of your tax money is re-distributed this way. Instead of being on the paying end, why not put yourself on the receiving end?

Other fund raisers get corporations or individuals to donate things that are "auctioned off for charity." To collect money or "things", use all laws, human empathy and good will available to you. If you are going to sell donated merchandise, you can probably get free space from a church. Your pitch is that they can ask their members for unwanted merchandise and furniture which you will sell for their benefit along with donations from other charitable organizations. All the organizations you deal with help publicize your event. Organize the raising or collecting of goods and services to benefit your good cause. Pay all expenses. Take your cut, as meager or generous as you want. Fifty percent is standard. Then pass on what's left to the people you want to benefit. Needless to say, it would fraud if you were blatant and the beneficiaries got nothing.

This is why religion stands out among good causes. As it is impossible to deliver money to God, it must all go to his servants on Earth. Of course, if you are using a church building rent-free to sell your things, be sure the people who run it will get a share. That will make them eager to cooperate with you on future sales.

You can certainly do some good in your hood and/or community by becoming a fund raiser for a good cause. You can also become very wealthy.

WHY YOU SHOULD CONSIDER NEVADA AS YOUR CORPORATE HOME

The State of Nevada offers business owners some very important advantages. Stop for a minute and think what you paid your state last year in State Income Tax. Nevada offers opportunities for greater profit through the absence of State tax on your business operations. These tax advantages are offered to all entities established in Nevada. Nevada State government officials have a very "business friendly" attitude. They feel the need to support a positive business climate and will do everything possible to help you build a successful business based in Nevada.

Many business operators active in the world economy are discovering the advantages of incorporating their business activities. Some advantages are greater liability protection, corporate deductions and privacy. Unfortunately, corporate law varies widely throughout the United States. In some places, it is so difficult to incorporate that you defeat any purpose or incorporating. There are, however, a few areas where corporate laws work to the advantage of the corporation, and to you as the owner.

The most common business entity is a corporation. Doing business as a corporation gives you asset protection and business privacy. It is very easy, and inexpensive to incorporate in Nevada.

You can operate your business in Nevada and live anywhere in the world.

In summary, the State of Nevada has the best corporate laws in the Unites States, including the lowest rate of taxation and the highest degree of privacy available in the United States. Major corporations and institutions such as Porsche North America and Citibank have discovered the Nevada advantage and set up their base of operations in the State of Nevada.

Nevada offers the officers and directors of a Nevada entity, a high degree of protection from lawsuits filed by disgruntled creditors or overzealous plaintiffs' attorneys. If you have ever considered incorporating, or if you are already incorporated, strongly consider the advantages that a Nevada based-operation has to offer.

Asset Protection is vital to your financial health. One of the most exciting, safe, and tax transparent business organization is a Limited Liability Company. Nevada is one of many states that recognizes this structure. The State of Nevada has adopted a Limited Liability Company law that offers all of the advantages of a corporate structure with the added advantage of tax transparency similar to that of S Corporations or Partnerships.

THE ADVANTAGES OF A NEVADA ENTITY

(In all cases where we use the word corporation, you may assume that this word may be substituted for Limited Liability Company or in certain situations, Partnership.)

What makes Nevada so attractive to corporations? Among other features, Nevada has the following to offer:

• Nevada has NO state corporate tax. Nevada has NO state personal income tax.

- Nevada has NO franchise tax. Nevada has NO taxes on corporate shares.

- Nevada has NO succession tax. Nevada corporate stockholders and directors are NOT required to be U.S. citizens.

- Stockholders and directors are not required to live or hold meetings in Nevada.

- Corporate meetings may be held anywhere in the world.

- Nevada allows corporations to determine what type of stock it will issue, including assessable, non-assessable and bearer shares.

- Nevada allows corporate by laws to be changed by directors.

- Minimum initial capital is not required.

- There are minimal reporting and disclosure requirements... Only the names and addresses of the corporate officers, directors and resident agent are public record. Our firm can provide nominees for the official directors/officers and will act as your registered office.

- Stockholders are not a matter of public record. As an owner or investor in a Nevada corporation, you may, if you choose, remain anonymous. You may appoint others to positions as directors and officers, and yet retain control of the corporation through ownership.

- One person may act as President, Secretary Treasurer, and Director of a Nevada corporation, fulfilling all disclosure requirements.

- Nevada allows corporations to conduct business at more than one office and also allows them to hold, purchase, mortgage, convey real as well as personal property in any of the states, or dependencies of the United States, the District of Columbia, or any foreign country.

- Nevada corporations can guarantee, hold, sell, assign, transfer, mortgage, pledge, or otherwise dispose of the shares of its capital stock, or bonds, securities, or evidence of indebtedness.

- Nevada corporations may purchase, hold, sell, or transfer shares of its own stock.

- Nevada corporations may issue stock for labor; services, personal property, or real estate, including leases and options. The directors may determine the value of any of these transactions, and their decision is final.

- Your corporate directors may, by majority resolution, designate one or more committees with a director or directors to manage the business of the corporation and have full powers.

- As of March 13, 1987, officers and directors of a Nevada corporation are protected from being held liable for the acts committed on behalf of the corporation or by the corporation.

- Nevada is the only state in the United States that does not have a reciprocity agreement with the Internal Revenue Service.

LET'S EXAMINE SOME STRATEGY

People have used their Nevada corporations and corporate bases to their advantage in many interesting ways. This statement is especially true for those who have corporations in other states and are losing from 3 to 12 percent of their income to state corporate taxes. (If you have a corporation qualified with the State of California, for example, and are using California as your corporate base, you are paying a minimum of $9,600 in taxes on every $100,000 of taxable income.)

Many have solved this problem by moving their corporate base or by setting up an additional corporation in Nevada.

You probably already provide your business with capital or services that it needs to function on a daily basis. With a little more imagination, a Nevada based corporation could be utilized to provide those very same functions.

Every business needs to be properly managed. If your Nevada Corporation were in the business of management consulting and services, it could contract with your present corporation to provide any management related service that the Nevada Corporation would require. Even though your present corporation has many business-related deductions over a period of a year, you could still end up with a taxable income of, say, $200,000. In the State of California, that amounts to $19,200 in state taxes. What if your Nevada Corporation were to bill your present corporation for its management services in the amount of $150,000? That management fee is a tax-deductible item reducing total home state taxable income to only $50,000.

Then you could, by forming another Nevada corporation, provide accounting services to your current corporation and bill it $45,000 in accounting fees, leaving only $5,000 in taxable California income. Get the idea?

To take advantage of this kind of technique, the accounting and management must actually be performed through your Nevada corporations. Furthermore, those Nevada services must be properly billed and invoiced. If you have someone appointed as officers and directors of your Nevada corporations other than yourself, no one can connect the ownership of the Nevada corporations (which is not public knowledge) with that of your current corporation (which most certainly is public knowledge).

Remember, Nevada has NO corporate taxes! Therefore, all the income that appears in your Nevada corporations may save you thousands of dollars in state taxes. This strategy provides you with a completely legal means of paying the least amount of tax on the money you have worked so hard to earn!

As important as the considerations of taxation is to businesses everywhere, we have found that the issue of liability is of equal concern to those who are involved in their own businesses. This is of particular importance in the economic times in which we live. For example, if you are an independent businessman and have built your business on consistent, reliable service, you have worked hard and want to make sure you're protected from unforeseen events. No one can predict how the courts will rule when someone goes after everything you have simply because they tripped on the sidewalk outside of your business.

You will be more secure if you form a Nevada corporation to which your present business is indebted. Because of the debt owed by your non-Nevada business, and the foresight you had to make a UCC-l filing in the applicable locals, the Nevada Corporation has the first lien on all of the assets. Now when a legal adversary wins a judgment that might close down the home state business, your Nevada Corporation takes possession of the assets to which it has a legal right.

Because you have incorporated in the state of Nevada, and have acted legally, you do not have to disclose your ownership of the Nevada Corporation. You have, therefore, protected all you have worked so hard to build.

There are other strategies for using a Nevada Corporation to your advantage which are far too numerous to mention. However, some of these techniques are ways to eliminate state capital gains tax, eliminate state sales tax and escrow fees on sale of real estate, freeze property tax base, and many more. Savvy hustlers are constantly discovering new uses for their Nevada based corporations.

When executing any corporate strategy, always check with your legal and tax advisors to tailor the strategy to your specific situation.

HOW TO LEGALLY PROTECT YOUR ASSETS ONCE AND FOR ALL!

Most people can benefit immensely by utilizing a strategy that many entrepreneurs and criminals alike have used for years. The strategy is based on two very simple principles: 1) A corporation is separate from the owner of the entity, and 2) The fact that true asset protection can only occur when the incentive to sue or in the case of criminal activity the opportunity for seizure is non-existent. Let's take a look at each of these points and then review the strategy to show you how everything works.

Corporations Are Separate from Their Owners

The most important thing to remember about any business entity is that it is separate from its owners. You are separate from your corporation, and your corporations are separate from one another. This is the very nature of the business entity, and it is the foundation upon which limited liability was built.

Because a corporation is an artificial person, you can do business with your corporation, and your corporation can do business with anyone else. This can include any other corporation you may own and or control. Your task in doing any type of multiple entity strategy is to maintain that separation. You separate you from your business by observing

33

the rules of corporate formality, by keeping your corporate records clear and up to date. If we recognize that a corporation is not you, then we are half way home to understanding the terrific benefits of this strategy.

This brings us to the second major point in our strategy. Asset protection can only occur when your adversary has no incentive to sue you or your business. It also occurs when the IRS, FBI, or any other agency can't seize assets they allege belong to you during a criminal investigation. How do we accomplish such a lofty goal? Well, let's look at something that may seem a little strange; poverty. While this may sound silly, ask yourself this question: How many destitute people are on the wrong end of multi-million-dollar judgments? When was the last time you picked up the morning paper and saw a headline which read, "Joe Homeless sued for 5.5 million"? On the other hand, you read every day about someone with assets being sued, or large corporations being hauled into court. Is that because the homeless person never gets into trouble? Not at all! It is probably because "Joe Homeless" isn't worth suing! Think about it. Would you bother suing somebody who you knew couldn't possibly pay a judgment? Not likely in this day and age when most attorney's work on a contingency fee basis – meaning they don't get paid unless there is something to take.

You may be thinking that it is all well and good to talk about using poverty as an asset protection tool, but poverty is no fun. You don't want to be poor. You own your own business so you can have financial destiny. Well, in this case you are.

The Strategy

Keeping these two important points in mind, let's take a look at the strategy itself. The benefit of the strategy is you will be able to protect your business and personal assets from litigious attacks and seizures, and you might have the potential to reduce your taxes.

For purpose of this report, we are going to call your home-state business 123, Inc. The other corporation in our example is going to be called ABC, Inc. ABC, Inc. is a corporation that will be formed in Nevada to provide a service to 123, Inc.

123, Inc. Takes A Loan

Let's say that your 123, Inc. corporation goes to the bank and borrows a significant amount of money. The bank is going to want collateral to guarantee repayment. Let's say that your corporation is required to offer all of its assets as collateral for the loan, and is then required to pay large sums of interest on the note, so large that it may have difficulty even making the payments. Therefore, 123, Inc. would always be in debt, and if the payments aren't made the bank can take everything 123, Inc. owns and pledged as collateral to re-pay the note. In essence, 123, Inc. could be wiped out. Perfect! Who would want to sue such a company?

Nobody, because even if they won, the bank gets paid off first, and then there's little likelihood of having anything left. Again, this accomplished the goal of "removing the incentive to be sued", but who wants to be in debt? Unless, of course, you were in control of the bank!

It is very possible through very proper planning and structuring that you can have your cake and eat it too. How? Because if the lending company was your own ABC, Inc. corporation, you have protected everything you own! You now have a home state corporation that has a terrible debt, and is unattractive to any adversary's lawsuit. But at the same time, you are calling all of the shots with its creditor. You have the best of both worlds. Even if somebody does sue 123, Inc., and obtains a judgment, what are they going to get? The same thing they would get if they sued "Joe Homeless" – only headaches. You, on the other hand, are in the driver's seat.

Even if you do not win the lawsuit you are judgment proof because ABC, Inc. is the bank. You have total control over it, and you decide what happens if 123, Inc. can't pay its interest, and you decide what happens if someone tries to take your assets from 123, Inc.

Remember that ABC, Inc. has the first lien on everything. Anybody trying to get at the assets at 123, Inc. must pay ABC, Inc. off first.

There's one more little detail we need to cover here, and that is paying interest on the loan made from ABC, Inc. This is a real loan, requiring a set interest rate to be set. Of course, interest on the loan is tax deductible and this would be true in 123, Inc.'s home state. But, if ABC, Inc. were located in an income tax Free State such a Nevada, how much income tax will it have to pay to its state? None! Thus, the more interest you can pay on the note, the more income you will move from your home state.

Summary

In short, the strategy involves two corporations. The first is your primary business, and for our example we called it 123, Inc. The other company will be a Nevada corporation, which we have called ABC, Inc.

123, Inc. borrows money from ABC, Inc. and as a result goes into debt. ABC, Inc. takes all of the assets of 123, Inc. as collateral for the loan, and files the necessary documents to perfect its security interest, such as UCC-1 financing statements for personal property, and mortgages or Deeds of Trust for any real estate. 123, Inc. pays interest to ABC, Inc. which reduces its state income tax, and ABC, Inc. has a first position on the assets of 123, Inc., making it a very unattractive lawsuit or seizure target.

That, in a nutshell, is the ABC-123 strategy.

TAX TIPS FOR CEOS

1. Set up a corporation: You can set up a medical expense reimbursement plan for yourself without including any employees. Your corporation can own and claim depreciation deductions on your car. Even if you are in business part time, you can set up a tax-sheltered retirement savings plan.

2. Work a swap of products or services at every opportunity. Both you and the other guy will save a lot in taxes. Neither of you will have as much recorded profit on a swap transaction. Hence, less tax.

3. Avoid employees: Have your work done by self-employed independent contractors and save on Social Security Taxes, Unemployment Taxes and Workman's Compensation Insurance.

4. If you carry an inventory, use the LIFO (Last-In-First-Out) method of valuing your inventory. Your non-deductible inventory will consist of the oldest items bought before price increases, and you will be deducting the highest-priced materials or merchandise.

5. When in doubt, deduct! The probability of an audit for a small business with less than $50,000 income is very low. Chances are your deduction will go through, and even if it doesn't, it will only cost you the tax you would have paid, plus a small interest charge. Just be sure you have a valid reason for your

deduction. But, do not get caught on a fraud charge. It is NOT worth it.

Note: The preceding tips are offered for general information only, and the reader is cautioned to seek competent tax counsel before using and of the above comments or information.

HOW TO START A BUSINESS WITH NO MONEY!

It's easy to assume that the only way a business will get off the ground is with major funding or the ability to raise ridiculous amounts of money. However, starting a business with no money (or very little) is entirely achievable with a little creativity and determination.

A Few Success Stories for Inspiration...

1. The Kingston Group, an American residential construction and remodeling firm, was started by two childhood friends with around $500 to cover licensing fees. Six years later it grew into a 3-million-dollar company.

2. Richard Bronson's probably one of the most inspiring stories for any entrepreneur. With just 300 euros from his mother, he started his magazine, 'Student', which was the catalyst for the entire Virgin Company. Today he's worth over 5.1 billion dollars.

3. Having pooled together $8,000 of their own cash and taking out loans, the three founders of Starbucks took their idea and ran with it, turning the company into a billion-dollar company almost 10 years later.

4. Billionaire founder of Topshop Philip Green started his

company with $20,000. He used the startup capital to import jeans from the Far East to sell to London retailers.

5. Using a $700 loan, John Paul DeJoria co-founded the Paul Mitchell line of hair care products and went on to become a billionaire businessman.

It's virtually impossible to avoid incurring any costs at all when starting a business, but there are a few ways to keep them to an absolute minimum and still get things to progress. Again, be creative and you will find ways to source cash. In 2008 one lady threw herself a birthday party and invited everyone she knew, asking them to donate $100 instead of a gift. And the two founders of Airbnb managed to raise 25 stacks for their business by buying cereal in bulk and fixing it with a clever name! They sold their Obama O's at a Democratic National convention for $40 each and managed to raise the cash they needed to fund the now billion-dollar company.

Also, be sure to SIMPLIFY your product/service and strategy and start off small rather than trying to launch with a huge line of services or products. It not only takes the pressure off significantly, but by concentrating on one product or service you'll save on initial cash outlay. Offering a single service or product in the beginning also enables you to focus on a defined target audience, building from there as the concept strengthens.

WHERE TO GET MONEY FOR YOUR START-UP BUSINESS!

1. Your Own Money, Otherwise Known as "Sweet Equity"

The idea is that, if you don't invest your own money into your business, why should someone else? The first thing most people say to this is, "I don't have any money to invest!" My answer to this is: get some, or make some!

If you can start your business without the need to borrow, you will be in a better position. You may wonder why I'm writing information on "funding," then telling you to get your own money. But the truth is, many people in business will need to raise money at some point in their journey, but getting in debt too much too soon is like carrying unnecessary weight. Debt is costly. It can be expensive to service and it could mean working under immense pressure. Be sure that you only get into debt as a last resort, not a first option.

So, how do you get money to invest in your business?

- Restructure the business to start with a smaller amount of money

- Use your savings

- Get a part time job

41

- Sell something of value and invest the money

- Sell part of your pension or cash in a part of your insurance policy

- Start a smaller business that will earn you the money for your desired business

2.   Customer's Money

One method to raise money for your business is having customers pay for your product or service in advance of creating/manufacturing/delivery. Let's examine two different examples of how this can work...

This works very well in the music business where fans can pay for an album in advance. The artist/label will then use the generated funds for studio expenses and manufacturing the CD or for enabling downloads. The music business even takes the principle further by offering different price points called packages. For example, you could buy the CD copy of the album for $10; CD plus T-shirt for $20; CD, T-shirt and other downloads for $50, etc.

One guy, who ran a property business, got clients to pay a deposit of $3000 each if they wanted him to find a property for them. This money was used to run their business. The only risk was that the amount was refundable after 6 months if they could not find a suitable property for the client. (Believe me, they made sure they always found a property the client would love!) This way, they had no need to borrow money and their cash position always looked great.

In reality, this can only work if you have established credibility with your clients or you have a product in high demand that they need. Either way, this is a very viable method of raising money that requires some thought!

Can you use this method to raise the money you need for your business? It is 100 times better than borrowing money!

3. Supplier's Credit Line

This can be a great source of raising money for a business. In simple terms, it means that the supplier allows you to buy products that you pay for later at an agreed date. The beauty of this type of financing is that you can order products, sell them, and then pay the supplier.

Just imagine you have a business that sells fashion products that cost you $100 each to make and sells for $200. If you got a credit line of $500 from the supplier, this ensures you could have 5 products to sell without the need to fork out any money. In this example, you can collect the 5 products, sell them for $1000, and then pay your supplier.

Another smart method could be combining "customer's money" with "supplier's credit line." Following the above example, you could ask the customers to pay a 25% deposit (which will be $50), and then use the credit line from the supplier. Due to the deposit, you will no longer need as much credit as before and you will still have products to sell to your customers and repay your creditors; all of this without the need to go to a bank to borrow a penny! In practice you might only be able to get credit from suppliers if they know you, like your business model, or a situation where they (the suppliers) are desperate for customers.

Finally, on the subject of supplier's credit, it is always a good idea to ask! A famous quote by Jesus says, "Ask and you will receive." Here is the deal; if you don't ask, you are guaranteed to get nothing. Never say no for the other person!

4. Family and Friends

The next best option available is money from capable family members and/or close friends. Do you have a rich uncle? Grandma and Grandpa are always willing to lend

MIKE ENEMIGO & SAV HU$TLE

money to one of their favorite children! A friend who has made a fortune in business could be more than willing to invest in the next big thing you have planned. This is a means of raising money that many people ignore. Don't!

Before we consider the process of actually getting money from family and friends, let us examine some of the advantages:

- Flexible

- Requires little or no security

- Lending can be interest-free

- Many offer longer repayment period than any financial institution

- May accept lower return on their investment

- May allow you to remain solely responsible

- May require a less detailed business plan

There are or could be some disadvantages, too. These are:

- Misunderstandings can affect relationships

- The person could be risking more than they can afford

- The person may demand their money back when it suits them, not the business

- The person may also want to get more involved in the business

Let us consider the process by exploring a few guidelines:

Is this money a loan, gift or investment: <u>Loan</u> means that, whatever happens to the business, you need to pay back the money at the agreed time with the stipulated interest which can be from nothing (zero interest), to whatever was agreed. <u>Gift</u> is just a blessing, free of any obligation to return the

44

funds. <u>Investment,</u> on the other hand, is clearly different. When a family member gives you money and it is termed an investment, be sure to mention <u>exactly</u> what that means. Investment means they could lose all the money if the business fails! Investment means they can have a say in how the business is run. Investment means they can earn interest as the business makes money.

What is the person's character or disposition to business: Family or friends who are risk adverse or have a low disposition to taking risks should not be considered as a good candidate to borrow money from. They could give you a gift, but avoid them giving you any loans or investments. Reason being, if things go wrong, it could ruin your relationship.

You should disclose all risks and worse-case scenarios. Particularly if it is an investment. Make sure this is not only done verbally, but written in the agreement.

Present a business plan: Even if a basic outline. It shows seriousness and professionalism that can put you in a good light with family and friends.

You should create a formal, written agreement: Since people have a way of forgetting agreements to their own advantage, drafting a simple agreement is still an essential part of raising money from family and friends. Write down the terms – type of money it is (loan, gift, investment); when payment will be made; interest rates, etc. Do NOT accept a verbal agreement only!

5. Crowdfunding or Fanfunding

Examples of these are kickstarter.com, indiegogo.com, gofundme.com, etc. What is this type of site and why is it popular? A crowdfunding service is an outline platform created to bring together project owners (Business, Charitable, or Personal projects), with those that might be interested in getting involved financially. Those getting involved can receive monetary compensation, product compensation, or just a personal satisfaction to know that a project they love is taking place and they have enabled its occurrence!

These sites are popular for a variety of reasons, some of which are:

- Convenience and the ability to be involved from your arm chair.

- The commitment is very minimal. Project investments can be as little as $10 for the first level involvement.

- In case you are wondering how the platform owners make money; they charge between 3-5 (typically) of the money collected for you.

Some of the plus sides for this kind of funding are:

- You do not need to pay the money back if the business fails, even though you stand to lose your reputation.

- You have the opportunity to receive funding from all over the world.

- There are no credit limits applicable by banks.

What it takes – points to note:

- Many people who hear about this type of funding get excited because they see it as a soft touch for raising money, but nothing could be further from the truth. Raising this type of funding requires hard work and extensive social media skills.

- Equally important is the need to create a compelling video (YouTube video) that will be used to market your project.

- Not everyone that places a project on the platforms raise the money they require.

- Those who create the necessary tools like videos and facebook pages, etc., and then go on to fold their arms in expectation will not see any fruit.

- This form of funding is highly competitive and donors have a huge number of choices.

- Some platforms will cancel the funding if the required target is not reached. Be sure to check the website's guidelines.

Those who are already savvy with online marketing will find it easier to raise money with this method. I also believe that those who have a project that touches the hearts of people should look towards this kind of funding, too. If you have a developed fan base, this type of funding could be the right campaign to look at. Be sure of one thing; this requires hard work and innovation to get the required funds!

6. Peer to Peer Lending

Examples are lendingclub.com, zopa.com, prosper.com, and fundingcircles.com. Important: if you have a good credit history, instead of running down to your bank, use one of these lending sites with rates as low as 6.54%.
The process is simple. Go to the site, get a quote, and understand the guidelines, make an application, and many will give you an initial response in 24 hours! Sometimes you might even get the money in your account within 3 days or, at the most, 3 weeks.
Here is what Funding Circle says: "Funding Circle is an online marketplace to help businesses find low-cost loans quickly, and investors get better returns. There are no middlemen, no banks, and no lengthy delays. By directly connecting people who want to invest money with vetted, established businesses who want to borrow money, we

eliminate the cost and complexity of the banking world. It's simple; we're better for business, better for investors, better all around." Visit them at www.fundingcircles.com

What to remember: This type of funding is only useful to those who have a good credit history. The rates are better, has no complexities and are very straightforward!

7. Banks – Credit Cards, Overdrafts, Bank Loans

Banks should be the last place to visit when seeking start-up funds. However, it is the first idea for most entrepreneurs. One small business bank manager says that, if they lend at all to a new business, the interest rate would be around 29! That's nuts! How can a business survive on that kind of interest rate? So in theory, rates advertised at 5-10 probably don't apply to a new business owner.

If you are intent on going to banks, then make sure you have been courting them before the day you need the money. By that I mean you must make sure all of your income passes through the account, and that you have periodical meetings with the manager to explain what you are doing and the plans you have in the future. (Remember, relationships are everything!)

If you show up to your bank manager for the first time just to ask for money, then he/she will have no choice but to lend to you based on your banking history only.

Some banks may ask you to complete a business plan based on their templates, but mostly this is merely a formality since they will lend whether you have a plan or not. Even if you have an LLC, most banks would require a start-up business to sign a personal guarantee for the loan.

Credit card interest rates range between 7-36. (I hear in Brazil it can be as high as 240, which simply means, "from now on, we own you!")

Some people have successfully used credit cards as a means of financing their business. However, running your business on a credit card can be very costly, so I suggest you just avoid this method if you can.

Your bank may allow you to overdraft, which means it allows you to use more money than you actually have in your account. It sometimes costs less than a loan or credit card as long as you are in the "black" more frequently than in the red. This is likely because the amount of interest charged varies with the level of overdraft facility used. So if you have a facility of $5000 and you have only used $2000 twice in the last 12 months, the interest you pay will be less than that of an individual with the same facility who has used $2000 ten times in the same period.

Overdrafts can be a good way to hold you over for a short period!

Grants

Grants are funding provided by the government or individuals to fulfill certain requirements within the society. These are different from loans because you are not required to repay such money, although where there is proof of mismanagement or misappropriation of funds, funders may request that the money be fully repaid.

Here are a few things to understand when it comes to grants...

• Typically grant funders do not care about your business, but only achieving the objective for which they are giving you the grant. Grant funding is set up to address community issues. So, there could be grant funding available for helping pregnant teens get back to work. If you have a training business and want to earn some money by getting a grant, you will need to set up a project that helps these teenagers get back to work and earn money doing this project. The money you earn can be spent as you wish, but the project outcomes must be fulfilled. In the end, what the funders want is for you to help them achieve their own objectives, although you get paid for it. One of the secrets for getting grants is making applications for delivering projects that are similar to what your business already has. Get it?

• Before making an application, you will need to research the funder in detail. If they specify the type(s) of projects they fund, make sure that is the kind of project you apply for. Do not waste your time applying for projects they will not fund. This only leads to frustration. Something equally important is to know when they receive applications. Some do all year round, but some have application deadlines.

• If you are a newbie, it will affect how much you can get. If you want big money, you will need to build a good track record. Do this by delivering smaller projects over the years, then increasing your application request. EVERYTHING takes time to build.

• Grant applications take an average of 3 months from application to money in the bank. This does not include resubmissions. Be aware that many individuals write as many as 3 applications before they get the money.

• Resubmissions are common, so don't let having to do it discourage you. Getting a rejection letter is not the end of the world! As a matter of fact, it is the beginning of the game. If you get a rejection letter you MUST call the funder and ask WHY, and find out what you can do to improve your application. 9 out of 10 times a resubmission has a greater chance of success.

8. Government Initiatives

Www.sba.gov/loans-and-grants is a helpful tool. Simply complete a list of 10 or so questions that helps you identify where you are and who can help you. Click submit, and out comes a list of options.

5 TIPS TO MAKE YOUR BUSINESS FUNDABLE!

1. Start Generating Some Sales Before You Go for Funding/Investment

There is nothing that makes a business (new or existing) more attractive than a business that generates sales. According to Brian Tracy in his recording of *Habits of Millionaires*, a study was conducted by Brad Street to determine why many businesses fail, and why others succeed. One of the results found was that, those businesses that had a high volume of sales succeeded, those that had no sales, failed. Point is, even new businesses need a number of sales to make their proposition attractive to potential investors. Sometimes you hear or read about the need for "traction." Traction is any number of sales that an investor can just come in and build upon.

There are 3 main reasons why you should have generated some sales before you start seeking funding:

• It proves to you and the investor that your business is financially viable.

• It means people out there are willing to pay for what you have.

• It gives you the confidence that your plan is more than an idea, but a workable venture.

The first challenge some people think of is that they need money generate their first sale(s). My response is this: structure your business in a way you can generate sales with your own money. If you don't, you are saying to investors, "Give me your money so I can try an idea that may or may not work." That is something most investors obviously don't like!

2. Have a Good Management Team

Your management team is a group of experienced individuals that are committed to steering your business to success. They can be paid, or unpaid. They can be physical or virtual. Your ability to gather the right group of people that compliment your own skills and have the right experience to strengthen the business' resolve for success, will influence your chances of raising funding.

Yet, the average new business owner does not even have or want a business mentor! That not only shows a certain arrogance, but also a lack of understanding. The saying that "two is better than one because they have a greater reward" is also applicable in business! Funders are aware that, no matter how brilliant your plan may be or how accomplished you are, you still need other people because you don't know everything, and two minds are always greater than one.

If you were looking to raise $1000 from a family member or friend, perhaps nobody really cares whether you have a management team or not. However, raising money from investors, who are unlikely to be related to you, is sure to get you asked many more questions.

Search for business owners. friends/family members with good business experience, mentorship schemes, and government development agencies for people who can act as part of your management team. *People invest in people!* Beyond you, are there any others within your business worth investing in?

3. Your Own Money

The general rule is that people are willing to put their money into your business after you have put yours in others, like banks, may even suggest that they are only willing to invest in your business the same amount you invest in it! When you have invested your own money in the business, you are simply demonstrating your commitment, belief and enthusiasm for the venture. Conversely, if you are not investing or risking any of your own money, why should someone else risk theirs?

4. Are You in A Hot Market?

There was a time when being involved in a dot com company was hot business. Then opinion swung to social media companies, especially after the boom experienced by Twitter. In my opinion, beyond a hot market is a hot product. Is your product hot? What I mean is, is your product in high demand? As common as the hair styling business may be in the city, a similar business in a new town with only 2000 people may be considered new and hot.

When funders perceive you have a hot product, they will be falling over each other to give you the money to run the business.

It is your responsibility to demonstrate whether you have a strong money-making product that is worthy of investment, and the way you can do this is by:

- Generating initial sales.

- Collating customer demand research data.
- Obtaining statistical information that supports the product.

5. A Solid Business Plan

Not just a few words on paper, but a plan that suggests your venture will work. Not just your opinion, but conclusions drawn from well researched operations. Not just some figures plucked out of the air, but numbers that are as close to reality as possible.

The plan of action you want to pursue (outlined in a business plan) will determine whether you get the money needed. Funding organizations have a variety of outlines and you must be prepared to cut and paste your existing plan to suit the outline they give you.

Warning: Even if you get someone to write your business plan for you, I suggest 2 things:

- First, do most the research yourself.
- Second, make sure you are very familiar with all the parts of the plan and are able to explain them in detail.

You will come across like a fraud if you are unable to answer any questions that relate to the business plan you have submitted. Go over the contents as many times as possible, do mock presentations to a trusted friend before you face the funders. Sometime one chance is all you will get with a particular funding organization!

Here are the 5 sections every business plan should have:

Section 1: Executive Summary – This is the first 2 pages of the plan, and it is a summary of all the other sections included.

Section 2: The Marketing Plan – This is the section that covers industry and sector overview, your competition, customers, products, etc. The whole plan you have.

Section 3: The Operations Plan – This section covers how you are going to do it; management team, business structure, insurances, etc.

Section 4: Financial Plan –This is where you include your cash flow forecast, profit and loss accounts, budgets, etc.

Section 5: Appendices – This section will include letters of recommendations, letters of intent, etc.

TOP 10 REASONS START-UPS FAIL TO GET FINANCED, PLUS SOLUTIONS

1. Funders Lack Understanding of The Business Sector

Most funders had specialized knowledge in a handful of industries and hopefully possess a wide range of business knowledge and experience. What this means is that funders may not have an in-depth knowledge of how your business sector or product works.

The problem is compounded when you as a business owner fail to provide enough information that educates the funders about your business and its sector.

So, rather than a funder tell you they lack understanding of the workings of your business, they will simply exercise their right to decline funding; bad news for you.

That said, here are 2 things to remember and do:

• Do not assume funders are specialists within your industry. Therefore, present all information in the simplest way. There is a saying that, if a 7-year-old can understand your business plan, you have done a good job.

- Always present a business case. This means your focus should be on establishing the workability and profitability of the business rather than displaying your knowledge of how your industry works. At the end of the day, funders want to know the business will make *money!*

2. Poor Relationship With Bank Manager

A majority of business owners trod along to see their bank manager at the point they have a financial need.

For many start-up business owners, the very first time they will set their eyes on their bank manager or write him/her by email is when they have a financial need! Think about this: how much would you trust a beggar or stranger who comes to your door to borrow $20 and pay you back in 10 days? You probably wouldn't trust him one bit. Now, if this person comes to your house or sees you in the street and chats with you frequently, you would be more inclined to lend them the $20, right? This is very similar to the way banks view your first business loan request. They think, "Who is this?" The only thing they can go by is your current bank statements, and if that fails to inspire confidence, then you are unlikely to get the funding from this source.

Here are 2 things to remember and do:

- If you ever think you will need your bank manager, I suggest you make regular visits and explain your desires and business goals with him/her. This creates a relationship that can help determine your future funding opportunities!

- Seek their advice. During your regular bi-yearly or quarterly visits, always ask for their contribution and advice in relation to the future of your business. As you execute this, he/she will be more likely to help you financially should the need arise.

3. No Good Track Record

One of the biggest frustrations of anyone seeking business funding is the thought of, "How can I have a track record if no one is willing to give me a start?"

So here are 2 things to remember and do:

• Track record is not only business experience. You can display a good track record that inspires confidence even when you have worked for someone else. It mainly depends on how you present the information. What I mean is that; work experience that relates to the business, presented in a strong and convincing way, can satisfy funders.

• Even if you have no work or business experience, get a volunteer role so you can start developing a track record.

4. Considered a High-Risk Sector

This means a situation where the funder considers your business sector as high risk. Believe it or not, most funders have a list of businesses they would rather not fund. Sometimes it is based on the failure rates of those business sectors/niches, and at other times it can be based on mere reluctance to enter that market. Whatever it is, you need to find out whether your section is considered as high risk, and then begin to work on dealing with said issue. (Understand that, just because a business is considered high risk, it doesn't mean it will never get funding.) Typical examples that I know of are music business' record labels, Internet businesses, etc.

Here are 2 things to remember and do:

- Be upfront. Tell them in the first 2 pages of your business plan (Introduction or Executive Summary) the risks associated with this business, and how you plan to resolve them. Never say there are no risks when it is glaring to funders that risks are eminent.

- Develop creative solutions. What you can start doing is listing all the risks associated with the business, and then ensure you have the right solutions for all of them. Gain the confidence of the funders by making them realize you have thought through the business process.

5. Lack of Experience Management

There is no such thing as a "self-made" man. You have heard the saying that no man is an island. I will go as far as saying that, the way God made us, we must be dependent on someone else. Has it ever occurred to you that every business is dependent on their customers? No matter how great you think your product is, if you don't have customers, it is simply a white elephant. In the same way, funders expect you to assemble a credible team who will provide advice, support, and management expertise on a day to day basis. Funders have provided funding based on the strength of the management team! So if you don't have a management team, or your management team is weak, funders may be reluctant to provide funding for your business.

So, here are 2 things to remember and do:

- Get the best management team. In my opinion, the best management team is one that has two groups of people; those who have general business knowledge, and the ones that have sector expertise. Think about the wealth of experience and knowledge that can be imported from another sector. I believe you need both types of people – sector experts and business experts.

- Find people that are willing to offer virtual services. There are management experts that will give you an hour a month free, and those that will defer payment for a year. Whatever the case, do not limit your search to your local area. Getting people from other states, or even different countries can be ideal.

6. Lack of Understanding of Funder's Requirements

It's shocking how much some business owners don't care about funder's requirements. Putting this bluntly, it is foolish not to consider the requirements of the funders. For example, before you approach anyone for money, you must be sure of a few basic things: a) types of businesses they fund; b) the format they require for application; c) any submission dates and deadlines; d) funding limits and so on.
Their needs, not just yours, should be paramount in your heart. If you fail to comply with their requirements, they are unlikely to consider your application. Do not be fooled into thinking *they* need *your* business. That may be true, but they also have thousands of applicants, and would rather give their money to someone who is compliant.

Here are 2 things to remember and do:

- Research their needs first. Do not engage in a blanket applications process. This means getting ahold of a long list of funders and just sending the same funding request to all of them – don't do that. It is better to research and just deal with a handful of funders.

- Make sure you give them what they want. Some funders want you to create their own business plan template. If this is the requirement, follow it completely. Do not simply attach your business plan, but rather tailor your plan to their requirements. In short, what I'm saying is; give them what they want, and how they want it!

7. Bad/No Credit Rating

Credit rating or credit scoring is one of the methods funders use to determine their decision to either fund or decline business funding. Much of what happens depends on the amount and accuracy of the information kept by the agencies used by the funders. In other words, if the information kept about you is wrong – for example, the records show that you defaulted on payments but you haven't – it is your responsibility to prove you did not default. If, however, the information is correct, you must give good reasons why this happened.

Here are 2 things to remember and do:

- Get and review your records. Before you start applying for money from funders, you should first get hold of your financial records kept by a reputable agency.

- Adverse report. If the information kept about you is adverse but true, you need to start working on a plan to resolve the debt. Most funders will overlook a default if you have a good reason and are doing something about it. Do NOT let funders discover your default! Tell them upfront!

8. Poor Banking Practice

This is applicable to those already trading in some shape or form and need additional funding. Poor banking practice is where the business owner fails to deposit all the amount of money generated from sales into the bank account. Let me explain; if you are making cash sales, there will be temptation to pay your bills straight from the money generated, without passing it through your account. This has a detrimental effect on your ability to raise money. The reason is, the bank records and your records will be different, since most of your cash sales will not be reflected in your bank statement. Therefore, if you want to get a loan from a bank or a funder that requested your bank statements, there will be some discrepancy between the sales you said you made, and the actual sales recorded. If you are the type of business that has made more cash sales than sales through the bank account, and you have failed to deposit the cash before spending it, your account will not look healthy enough for a loan/funding!

Here are 2 things to remember and do:

• Pay all money through your bank, even before you pay your own wages. Pay all monies into your bank account *first.*

• Make sure your records are the same. Your bank records and your sales records should be the same!

9. Lack of Perseverance

.It was reported the Colonel Sanders visited about 50 states looking for funding before he got money for his Kentucky business. The Beatles went to many record labels before signing to Parlophone. Lack of persistence and perseverance has robbed many business owners of the opportunity to secure the funding they need to get their business going. People always ask me how long it takes to raise money. I tell them an average of one month if you are getting money from family or a bank, 3-6 months from government agencies, and about 18 months from business angels! But a better answer is... however long it takes to get the money! The length of time is irrelevant. It's about getting what you need, and that should be your focus.

Here are 2 things to remember and do:

• Keep going until you get it. If it means going to all the funding sources you can find, then do that! Never stop! Never give up!

• "No" does not mean never. Many people think no means it will never happen. Not true. Sometimes "no" means there's more you need to do, or "this is not for us."

10. Poor Business Plans, No Evidence of Market Research, & Poor Evidence of Ability to Repay Loan

Nearly every funder will require you to produce some form of a business plan. The actual size and intricacy will vary from one funder to the next. However, having a solid business plan that details the essentials will get you half way there. A good business plan should have the following five categories: Summary/Introduction, Marketing Plan, Operational Plan, Financial Plan, Appendices. Covering the areas in detail will ensure you understand your market and have the right mix to enable success and repayment of the amount borrowed/invested.

Here are 2 things to remember and do:

• Can you repay? Make sure your cash flow and profit/loss account communicate the ability to repay or provide a timely exit strategy.

- Write a well-researched plan.

UNDERSTANDING THE PSYCHOLOGY OF INVESTORS!

It may surprise you to know that most people who seek funding do not care about the funders at all. As a matter of fact, some prospective business owners believe the funders owe them and should provide the funding without many questions.

The other extreme is those business owners who think funders (especially rich: individuals) have more money than sense. These business owners think they can say anything; even make ridiculous claims, and the funders will be no wiser.

Both are extremely wrong. Be sure that most people who have money, do so because they are smart people. They have dealt with so many unscrupulous individuals that they have become a very good judge of character. Besides, the wealthy are so paranoid of people taking advantage of them, they have developed strong antennas to detect the slightest bit of untrustworthiness.

With this in mind, you must understand what the funders are looking for so you can tailor your approach to achieve the goal of getting the funding you want.

Here are 5 tips:

1. Funders Want To Make More Money

The reason why people invest in businesses is to make more money. Even when most government agencies give out loans, they are still hoping to get that money back, with interest. Be sure to approach your potential investor with a business plan that will be a financial win-win for you and *him/them*!

Thinking this way will not only radically increase your chances of getting the funding you want, but change your mentality and business in the process!

Even though funders know that not all businesses will make millions, they still hate losing money!

2. They Want You To Tell Them The Risks, And What You Have Done About It

Eric Ries, author of *Lean Start-up*, started a pitch by saying how he's had so many businesses, but many of which failed. Shocking! How can a businessman start with that kind of statement? The reality is that, failure breeds success! First, he was transparent, then followed it up by telling the audience how he made millions in business *successfully.*

I once heard that you should lay out the risks plainly in the executive summary, and what you plan to do to overcome them. Everyone, including funders, know there are risks involved. Trying to cover up, or suggesting there are no risks at all, will make you come off deceptive. Know the major and minor risks and deal with them openly.

3. Funders Want Winners – Star Businesses

It's said that four out of five businesses funded by VCs and Angels do not produce as the investor/funder hopes. But, the fifth one does exceptionally well, and it makes up for the four so-so businesses.

Funders are always on the lookout for "star" businesses. Is your business exceptional? Funders are looking for such!

Take government agencies, or those who offer soft loans (loans that require less formalities and credit worthiness). They still require those businesses that do exceptionally well, because that will help promote their service!

4. Funders Want To Know Who Is Behind the Company

Who are the management team? And, just so you know, having an unknown person a part or your management team is better than having nobody at all. However, the more you are able to persuade a brand-named person to be a part of your management team, the better your chances are of obtaining funding!

5. They Want a Compelling Pitch

When you have the opportunity to present your business idea to funders, it must be excellent on the first take! Have you ever watched Shark Tank or Hatched? You will notice that, those who do not have a compelling pitch or are unable to answer basic questions are less likely to impress the Sharks.

If you follow what has been written in your executive summary, you are likely to give a compelling pitch. Your pitch must include the following:

- Your background and business experience.

- The idea and what it is you're selling.

- How you plan to reach the niche market.

- The number of sales already generated.

- Expected sales and profits over the next 1-3 years.

- How much you want, when and how you plan to pay it back.

Get money!

CONTRACT SECRETS!

How To Be Sure Your Contract Isn't Read...

If someone signs a contract, they are bound to it, unless they were illegally forced to sign it. But you don't have to use force to insert something into a contract. Do what the insurance and credit card companies do:

PRINT PERTINANT PROVISIONS IN EXCLUSIVELY CAPITAL CHARACTERS, EMPLOYING SAN SERIF TYPEFACE (COMPLETELY SANS DIMINUTIVE APPANDAGES, CURLICUES, WHORLS). MOREOVER, LIKEWISE JUDICIOUSLY EMPLOY THE APPLICATION OF LENGTHY, WORDIER, MORE TROUBLESOME WORDING OF EXTENUATED READERSHIP DIFFICULTIES. SUNDRY SCIENTIFIC EXAMINATIONS HAVE NOW IRREFUTABLY ESTABLISHED WITH FIRMNESS OF COMPLETE CERTITUDE THAT PARAGRAPH COMPOSITIONS PRINCIPALLY COMPOSED OF CAPITAL CHARACTER FORMATIONS AS DISPLAYED HEREIN RESULT IN THE LIKLIHOOD OF SUCH FORMULATION BEING SUBSTANTIALLY OF INCREASED DIFFICULTY TO DECIPHER.

Did you fall asleep? You most likely didn't read the whole paragraph. The use of all capital letters, wordy, convoluted prose... this is how to slip something into a contract, or even an advertisement that you don't wish people to read.

Never Sign Personally...

Try never to sign a contract, lease, bank loan, agreement, or other document. If something goes wrong, you'll be personally responsible. And maybe sued. Rather, you should always bargain to have your corporation do the signing.

It doesn't matter if it's a small home business or a million-dollar corporation. Make your corporation look big and impressive, and tell the other party's lawyer that you never sign personally. Don't give in on this and give your signature only as a last resort.

Use Ready-Made Contracts...

Instead of paying a lawyer big buck to draw up contracts or agreements, most contracts you will need can be bought at a stationary or supply store. You can even buy inexpensive computer software containing dozens of ready-made documents, and some can even be downloaded from the internet for free.

However, you will need a lawyer if the contract is complicated, or if you are dealing with a sneak. Or if his lawyer or adviser is one.

THE TAKEOVER: HOW TO TAKE OVER A GOING BUSINESS WITH ZERO "CASH"!

Here is another secret that can make you a boss, and wealthy, virtually overnight: Taking over a "going" business. The reason is because when you take over a business, you also take over the salary of the owner, and that can often be as much as 150 stacks yearly.

To get started, you should look for a business that is in deep trouble; one that is about to go bankrupt. Many of these businesses can be acquired with little or no down payment. They could be manufacturing, service businesses, real estate-based businesses, or almost any other type.

Why would someone offer a business for zero cash down? Here's why: The owner of a failing business will be glad to get out from under his bills and headaches. He's burned out, and believes the business is beyond saving. And that finding a buyer for a heavily indebted business will be extremely difficult.

There are plenty of these cash-free takeovers available and often advertised. What you have to do is look for them. Search through business ads in newspaper classifieds, trade magazines, and online. Also check with local business brokers and real estate agents who handle business sales.

Find Out Everything: Once you have found a suitable business, you must get all the details concerning it. For instance, you will have to find out how much the business owes and to whom, the value of the building and property itself. What you are looking for are the firms whose inventory and assets are higher than their debts. You must also consider the sales income and expenses in operating the business. Look for such things as, the gross sales, selling and labor costs, taxes, and so on. This information can come from the firm's account books, income tax returns, or from an accountant's certified statement.

Make An Offer: Explain your belief to the owner that you think you can turn the business around and make it profitable, but it will take at least two years. Since this is your plan, here is a typical offer you make to the owner:

- Zero cash down

- Offer him promissory notes

- No note payments for two years

- Offer to pay all the debts of the company

- Now be sure to have your lawyer draw up a proper sales agreement before buying. You should also try for an arrangement to pay the attorney's legal fees from business funds, not your own pocket.

If you find that you absolutely must give the owner a nominal down payment, you can use any of the capital raising methods in this book, or the Hood Millionaire's Money Manual. However, you must insist on paying the bulk of the price with promissory notes. And you should insist that payments do not begin for a year, preferably two. You will need that long to turn the business around and show a profit.

Once you have acquired your sick business, you must take steps to make it profitable. The first step is to deal with the creditors. Here is what you do:

Set up an appointment with each creditor to discuss the firm's indebtedness, explain to them that you have just taken over the business and you would like to pay off all the debts as soon as possible. Tell them the business has no cash at the moment but that you hope to start showing a profit in six months to a year. Your strategy is to convince the creditor to accept a reduced settlement of the debt.

First, try to get a debt reduction of from 30 to 70 percent from the total debt. You must also insist that no payments begin for at least one year. Your third request will be for a long-term repayment plan – 10 years, if possible. Once your creditor has accepted the offer, make it legal by getting him to sign an agreement. Through this maneuver alone, you will have reduced your debt by 30 to 70 percent, lowered payments by getting payoff time extended, and received complete debt relief for one year.

Taking care of the business debts has helped substantially. It is now in a far better position to recover from its sickness, but you don't stop here. You can also:

1. Sell off excess inventories (finished goods or raw materials).

2. Sell part of your production machinery.

3. Sell more stock in your firm.

4. Sell a division or separate department.

5. Split your company into separate firms and sell the stock.

6. Make any other cost cuts you can: Reduce payroll, find cheaper supply sources, eliminate waste, etc.

7. Eliminate products, services, or accounts which are

marginally profitable.

8. Study how to increase sales and locate new markets.

Incredible as it sounds, there are many businesses that can be saved through these methods. All too frequently owners are completely unaware of the true value of their business. In many cases, the owner has exhausted his operating capital and credit through mismanagement. Your offer allows him to recoup some of his investment, and your offer may be the only one he gets!

The Corporate Takeover: You can use a variation of the promissory note method by offering the owner corporate stock as a down payment, or even as full payment if the owner is really desperate. Assuming you set up a corporation with ten other investors, the owner would be assured of a sales potential of 10 customers for his stock once the business gets going.

BO$$ STATUS: A GUIDE TO ENTREPRENEUIRAL LEADERSHIP!

When I think of the best leadership, I am moved and humbled. Great leaders inspire and create meaningful, lasting opportunities and new ways of thinking. They believe in change. They have an impact on the future.

Like many roles in life and business, being a true leader is a calling. Either you're a great one, or you're not. Think of those who have changed the expected, like Picasso, Plato, Thelma and Louise, Socrates and Tom Brady.

Those are the ones that blaze new trails without fear, without worry and without a second thought to what other people think. They have a singular vision and a singular course. They dare to challenge ideas with a nimble flick of the throttle, changing directions as easily as batting an eye. They see things others do not. They take risks. They are entrepreneurs. Just like you. And if you doubt that fact, sit back and have a read.

Leadership is your contribution and your service to your company. It's your survival, and that of those you lead. It will be your legacy, and your company's legacy. It is what makes you great versus what lets you fail or, worse, be average.

Ask anyone in the armed forces – especially those operating in the battlefield – about leadership, and they will be telling. It's usually along the lines of: "I am leading you to keep you alive. I lead for you, and I lead to make you better."

The point is: Leadership is never about you – it's about them. And how you lead says a lot about your company and a lot about you. And if you're not good at it... damn, that's bad.

Those who are true leaders will lead their teams to victory and inspire them to be great. I've worked with that type, and I've worked with leaders who are managers and mostly check timecards. The difference is epic. Leadership is not about bossing or being in control. Nope. It is that belief that you and your team are destined for something special. It is your ability to inspire excellence in others.

Any organization, company, product, magazine or brand will always, always, every single time, take on the essence of its leader. If you lead with courage, clarity and fearlessness, then that's what your brand will stand for. The same goes if you are a careless, hopeless, entitled brat.

I've succeeded and I've failed as a leader. And the lesson is this: When you lead with purpose and vision, you will succeed. When you lead out of fear, you will fail.

BO$$ STATUS: HOW TO BUILD YOUR TEAM

7 Keys to Team Development and Success!

Being a phenomenal leader isn't about the leader – it's about the team. To create a successful and innovative team, you need to be flexible and able to collaborate with team members who may be your complete opposite. It's about finding their strengths and focusing on how to leverage their unique talents to improve the entire team.

Here are the seven keys for team development you should keep in mind to ensure the success of your team:

1. Thoughtful Recruiting...

The process of recruiting new team members cannot be rushed. To find the best employees for your team, you need to first determine your business' unique needs. Then, you should refuse to settle until you find the perfect fit between your company and a potential employee. It can help to develop specific competencies that your next hire needs to possess. Establishing these criteria, before you accept applications and interview all candidates several times to ensure they fill the needs of the position, are essential to the team-building process.

2. Initial Training...

As a leader, you should make the development of individual team members your top priority. Leading is more than teaching the mechanics of a role. You should show your enthusiasm and teach your employees how to maintain high-energy attitudes. Business school teaches the rules, but it doesn't teach how to be a top producing or innovative employee. You may consider designing a proprietary training program that's progressive and hands-on. Your employees already have the professionalism and passion, they just need to learn the correct mentality and receive support while they build the business.

3. Promoting Collaboration...

All of your team members have unique strengths and weaknesses. Use them to your advantage. By placing each team member in a position that harnesses strengths and down plays weaknesses, you ensure that everyone is successful and able to reach their full potential within the team. Leverage your talent pool to its peak productivity and encourage collaboration. This is the key to innovation.

4. Having A Passion for People...

Value your people more than the processes. Have fun. Get out of the office! Celebrate your employees' work and their personal successes. Once you understand your team members and what they enjoy, you'll start to feel like a family.

5. Consistent Coaching...

Coaching your team goes beyond training. It's an ongoing

conversation that will continuously increase productivity and team engagement. Meet with your team and individual employees regularly, either weekly or monthly, to ensure you are identifying obstacles or opportunities as they arise and addressing them directly. Dangle the carrot in front of your team. Keep energy high by creating goals of achievement for additional possibilities.

6. Maintaining Accountability...

Once you create goals for your team, clearly communicate your expectations. For example, ask your team members to work to their strengths while focusing on the top 20 percent of their most impactful and income-generating activities. Holding yourself and your team accountable to these standards will keep you on track while making you more relatable.

7. Leading By Example...

Strive to intentionally make a difference in your team members' careers. Be deliberate. If business is slow and calls need to be made, don't be afraid to do the hard things to encourage others. It takes cognitive control and discipline to bring positive energy to the table every day, but it will pay off and your reputation will thank you. Focus on productivity and profitability, and remember: high-impact priorities lead to critical advantages.

The team development process isn't over once you hire your dream employees. Building an innovative and collaborative company requires an on-going commitment to your individual team members. Bring a high-energy attitude to the table every day and encourage your team members to do the same. If you encourage them and put your trust in them, they will deliver for you and your bottom line.

Remember, to be a successful leader, you must inspire your team to greatness. If you motivate them to be great, they will take care of your company. Develop a positive workplace culture and you won't have to worry about your employees. They will reward you and take care of your bottom line.

BO$$ STATUS: HOW TO ENCOURAGE YOUR TEAM!

Encouragement. It sounds like such a small thing. Subtle. Cute. It's what we do with timid kittens.

But encouragement isn't cute – it's fraught and powerful. When you're encouraging, you're instilling courage. That's huge. And that's hard. And it's way more compelling than motivation.

Motivation doesn't depend on circumstances. Motivation is for people who are already inclined to try to succeed.

The commencement addresses that go viral are always more encouraging that they are motivational. The speakers recognize a specific concern – like needing to get a job or facing an uncertain future – and discuss ways it can be overcome. They don't offer some vague challenge like "surmounting an obstacle" or "seizing upon your dreams" or "surmounting your dreams by seizing upon an obstacle" or whatever the current motivational clichés are. Do these addresses involve motivation? Yes. Are they "motivational" in that unctuous way that motivational things are? No. Commencement addresses make listeners accountable. Encouragement inherently involves accountability – and not just for the one being encouraged. The encourager is accountable, too.

How To Encourage...

Praise the actual. If you read all the research on motivation, it pretty much comes down to this: Praise works better then criticism.

We all have an emotional tank. It works like the gas tank of a car. There has to be way more tank-filling than tank-draining.

Acknowledge the potential. Encouragement involves the acknowledgement of a negative thing – that the people being encouraged don't know they're not doing (or trying to do) but you think they should be doing. They might think they're doing just fine, that they're being appropriately effective and ambitious. Encouragement often involves bursting a confidence bubble.

To be encouraging, you must believe two things to be true. One, the person is not trying hard enough, which is probably not something the person wants to hear; and two, if the person tried, he or she could do great things, which is good. The key to encouraging is to deliver the bad news in a way that doesn't force the person to dwell on inadequacies. The key to encouragement is tact.

Start off by telling them their strong points and acknowledging their efforts and talents. 'You're extremely creative and you're brilliant, and you're wonderful at coming up with new ideas.' And then from there you can say, 'I would love to see you be able to segue that into a more organized manner.' It's very easy for people to kind of lose track of what they're doing right and what they're doing wrong.

Challenge specifically. You motivate generally. But you must encourage specifically. This holds the person accountable. 'You should ask this person for help.' 'You should go after that job.' 'You should consider switching to this career.' Like that.

For example, 'I think you have the potential to be a fantastic leader and to have three people work under you...but in order to do that, I think we need to improve upon your time-management skills, your organizing skills,' vs. coming at them saying, 'You're disorganized.' Approach it from a potential route.

Why It Matters...

Encouragement means empowerment. A lot of time it comes down to guide autonomy. So, on one hand, we know from research that people are much better at work when they feel empowered, which consists of having meaning on the job, a sense of autonomy, a sense of confidence, and also an impact on what you do and the people you're trying to help. Yet you don't want to feel so autonomous that you have no direction. It's one thing to feel autonomous in terms or your motivation, but it's another thing to be autonomous and go in the wrong direction.

You have to discourage before you encourage. That challenge is scary – for both parties. But the reward is sweet. Not only have you helped someone achieve a goal; you've helped someone achieve a goal that he or she didn't previously have. That's not merely motivational – that's magical. You're a wizard, a coach, a seer and (if we're being honest) kind of pain, all at the same time.

Key Technical Matters...

Encouragement has two parts: Pointing out potential and challenging the person to succeed at a specific goal.

You have to point out what it is to believe the other person could do. And you have to challenge him or her to do it. Which is why it's so much more meaningful than motivation.

You can motivate anyone. You can encourage only someone you actually believe in.

- Encouragement requires specificity.

- You don't encourage someone to succeed. (That's motivation.) You encourage someone to succeed at a specific task or job.

- You don't encourage people to "do it." You encourage people to do that thing you think they are prepared to do but has never occurred to them.

- Behind every successful person is someone who said: "You should try this. I think you'd be good at it. And here's how you should try."

That last part is important. Encouragement without guidance isn't encouragement. It's discouragement. "Here's what you're not doing! Bye!"

When you encourage, you don't just change how people work. You change the way they perceive their abilities. Which changes their careers. Which changes their lives. Which is a really big deal.

BO$$ STATUS: HOW TO BE A BETTER BOSS

One of the great things about being a boss is that you can delegate various types of tasks to other people instead of having to do them yourself. This may sound like a rather cavalier statement, but it's true. As a manager, to do your job efficiently and effectively, you must delegate various types of tasks to your staff. If you don't delegate, you will be overworked and your staff will be underutilized. In fact, you do a disservice to your staff if you don't delegate because this inhibits your staff's ability to learn new things and grow as professionals.

Like all management activities, delegation must be done in a thoughtful, ethical and forward-thinking manner. To that end, consider the following tips when delegating tasks to your staff, contractors, vendors and others.

1. Clearly define what can and cannot be delegated.

As a boss, be mindful of what should and should not be delegated. For example, specific tasks may contain proprietary information that should not be shared at your staff's organizational level. There are also tasks that your team members may not be qualified to perform, thus setting them up for failure. Lastly, don't just dump unwanted activities onto your staff to get them off your plate. Your team will eventually figure this out and it will hurt your credibility as their manager.

Delegation in a powerful tool to maximize your team's productivity, enhance their skill set, help them grow professionally and free you up to perform higher level tasks. All that said – make sure you are delegating the right tasks for the right reasons.

2. Create a prioritized delegation plan.

Now knowing what to delegate, your next step is to develop a plan outlining what tasks should be delegated to which staff member. When determining who gets which tasks, you should consider the following:

- Who is fully qualified to perform the task?

- Who could perform the task with proper instruction and mentoring with the goal of enhancing their skill set?

- Who should not be given the task because of their professional weaknesses?

- Who deserves the task based on seniority, past performance and relevant considerations?

- The visibility and importance of the task to your department and/or company.

Delegating the right tasks to the right people is not always easy or popular, but if you do it with transparency, fairness, consistency, and for the good of the company, your staff will learn to respect your decisions.

3. Provide clear instructions.

There is nothing worse than being delegated a task, not given instructions on how the task should be performed, not told what is expected, working diligently to complete the task, and then being told it isn't what they wanted. Give specific instructions as to what needs to be done and your expectation of the ending result. This combination of instructions and expectations provides the correct delegation framework and establishes criteria as to how your employee will be judged when the task is completed.

4. Provide a safety net.

When delegating tasks – particularly if it's a new experience for the employee being assigned the task – as the boss, you must be willing to provide an appropriate level of management support to help assure success, for both the employee and the task.

A safety net is an environment of help and protection by:

- Providing the needed resources.

- Allowing time to perform the tasks.

- Helping employees navigate company politics.
- Provide instructions on how tasks should be performed.

5. Let go and allow people to do their work.

If you delegate a task and then micro-manage it to the extent that you have actually performed the task yourself, it's not delegation. Neither should you totally divest yourself from the delegated task because, as the boss, you are still ultimately responsible for all work performed within your department. The trick is to walk that fine line between being overbearing and non-participatory.

6. Be mentoring and instructive.

This step provides direct instruction and advice to the person performing a specific delegated task. This type of task-based instruction is a "learning moment," namely, just in time training on how to perform a specific task or how to deal with a specific situation. The level of instruction and advice to be provided should be based on the combination of the person's specific experience and the task difficulty and political ramifications.

7. Give credit to those doing the work.

As a boss, you should adhere to the philosophy of "it's the team's success or my failure." This philosophy causes you to raise the visibility of your staff's good work within the organization which is motivating them and helps instill loyalty in your staff toward you.
This approach also helps remind you that you are ultimately responsible for both your team's growth and your department's productivity and performance.

8. Actively solicit feedback from your team.

Asking the members of your team if they believe you have delegated the right tasks to the right people has the following advantages:

• Helps you grow as a boss/manager by learning how you are perceived as one.
• Helps improve your team's performance by providing you with insights on better ways to delegate.

SCARED MONEY DON'T MAKE MONEY!

As human beings, we are emotionally wired. Some of those emotions like love, faith and enthusiasm are positive. The emotions of fear, jealousy, and greed are negative. Both positive and negative emotions are here to serve us. They're wired into our being and are meant to be used together.

I'm no psychologist, but I do know through my life's experience that leaning toward the positive side of the emotions is immensely powerful. Any particular negative emotion can be dangerous, especially if it becomes a habit. A little greed can make you financially free and will enable you to help others. But too much...and you've got a problem. A little fear keeps you alive. Too much fear keeps you stuck. With this foundation, let's explore why "Scared Money Doesn't Make Money."

Fear

Have you ever been backed into a financial corner? I have! And my research has revealed that most successful entrepreneurs have as well. You know the feeling of looking at that UN-paid pile of bills, dodging the phone calls, juggling the credit card payments. This is a critical moment in time for your business. It will define your success or lead to your downfall. You can either make it a stepping stone to bigger and better things, or you can choose to let it become a lifetime of "coulda, woulda, shoulda, if only I knew" thinking. And the key that unlocks wisdom and success comes only from the school of hard-knocks, by taking bold action – in spite of fear.

What about the world around you?

Go against conventional thinking. In the last two years, most the economic talk has been about "The Great Recession." I'll make a prediction that somewhere down the line the talk will be about "how good the economy is." It's just a cycle of life and you can't control it. So what should you do?

Do almost nothing and control what you can. I'm not saying you should sit around. What I'm saying is that you and I must not let the "masses" of people who are not leaders and entrepreneurs influence our thinking and – more importantly – our actions. We must influence the masses! Of course, looking for opportunities in both boom and bust is a good thing. You'll always have the most control of the actions you decide to take. Keep working at your goals. Keep testing things. Keep innovating.

Don't Stop Marketing!

Too many business owners think cutting the marketing budget is the answer. It's not! It's scared thinking! When your prospects and customers are more inclined to hang on to their money, you just need to work harder and smarter at ethically persuading them to want what you have to sell. That means increasing your communication and maybe even your marketing budget. Remember, you and I don't get ahead by subscribing to conventional wisdom!

Back in the "Great Depression" there were companies who caved in to conventional wisdom and stopped marketing. Those companies didn't survive. Then, there were those companies who pressed on and innovated. Many of them are still around today.

Keep Learning!

One of the best things you can do for yourself is to become a life-long learner. As a business leader, one of your jobs is to turn your ideas into profits. Bringing an idea to life and watching it grow is an amazing thing. But where do ideas come from?

Your mind is like a manufacturing plant. To turn out quality products, a manufacturing plant needs quality raw materials. Your mind needs quality information. By giving your mind quality information like this report, good books, seminars and inspirational audio on a daily basis, you'll give it the raw materials it needs to produce quality ideas that you can act on.

Strengthen Your Posture!

I'm not a huge fan of the whole "fake it till you make it" mantra. I believe in mental preparation and mental/physical rehearsal. But whether you fake it till you make it or thoroughly prepare, strengthening your posture is key. Whether you've got some temporary money problems or you're feeling a little UN-easy about the economy, you can't let it show. If you do, people will take advantage of you. You'll get paid less. So how do you strengthen your posture?

Strengthen your posture by going back to the basics. Be mindful of your body language. Since most communication is not based on words alone, think about how you walk, how you stand and the inflection in your voice. Maintain eye contact. Also keep in mind not to try too hard because others can sense that too! Be yourself, you deserve success!

Find Your Passion!

I think a lot of people who are filled with the wrong kind of fear are simply not passionate about what they're doing. Of course, this doesn't mean that passion will erase fear. The fear will still be there, but it will be the right kind of fear. When you are passionate about your business, you'll be able to keep your fear in check. Your fear will be an asset and not a liability. Passion will help you take bold action toward your dreams.

Finally, let the following quote and acronym remind you of how important it is to move boldly in the direction of your goals...

"Boldness has genius, power, and magic in it." – Johann Wolfgang von Goethe

And...

B.A.C.E. It stands for Bold Action Creates Energy

CEO BANKRUPTCY SECRETS!

Most people and companies seeking the protection of the United States Bankruptcy Courts do not plan for their bankruptcy but generally wait until the "wolf" is at the door huffing and puffing in the form of creditors, usually lien creditors holding a mortgage or judgment. Bankruptcy planning is an important aspect of preserving control over one's assets, especially with a view toward transferring ownership of the assets significantly in advance of the bankruptcy so that creditors and trustees appointed by the bankruptcy court cannot reach them through avoiding powers. This is the reason why many wealthy people can successfully go into bankruptcy and come out controlling most, if not all, of their assets.

Bankruptcy no longer has the negative connotation it once had, and many younger people are seeking protection of the bankruptcy court without the feeling of being stigmatized that older people feel. Years ago, only people who failed in business or in their personal lives sought protection of the bankruptcy court. Today, through proper planning with one's attorneys and accountants, bankruptcy may enable one to actually reorganize his/her/its life to such a point that he will be stronger as a result. It is also a useful tool for those planning retirement, especially in Florida, and they may be able to fund their retirement program through an organized dissolution of their business.

It is very important to realize that there is nothing illegal in bankruptcy as long as one plans it properly and is honest regarding the schedules and bankruptcy petition, which must be signed under oath. As long as one does not lie about assets, and reveals truthfully all assets and obligations to the bankruptcy court, there is nothing wrong with using the law to one's advantage. This report is not intended to be a guide for a person to plan or execute a bankruptcy without assistance of counsel, but merely gives suggestions on the directions a person may wish to take with advice or counsel.

Example

The person planning the bankruptcy in this example will be called Mr. A, a man who owned a restaurant as a sole proprietor and who was borrowing money from family members to keep up with his lease payments on the restaurant. Family members had also guaranteed the lease, so they were in financial jeopardy along with Mr. A. Mr. A also had a partner who wished to open a wine and cheese shop approximately twenty miles from the current restaurant, and believed that this would be a money generating venture which would get both out of debt. They were both first advised to become incorporated, which they did. Two corporations were established, one for the restaurant and a separate one for the wine and cheese shop. Within one year of the opening of the wine and cheese shop, the business anticipated by the partners did hot arise and the corporation operating the wine and cheese shop was deeply in debt. Unfortunately, both individuals had guaranteed the lease and were several months in arrears.

Mr. A and his partner returned to counsel for advice, who promptly suggested that the corporation would be wise to liquidate, but the equipment would best be moved to safe keeping since they did not trust their landlord. They were advised that the equipment would become part of the bankruptcy estate, but that the other corporation might be able to purchase it for ten cents on the dollar for its use. The wine and cheese shop then began to sell off its inventory in the ordinary course of business, and when its inventory was very low, closed the doors and moved the equipment for safekeeping. The corporation filed for protection under the bankruptcy code, but the landlord filed suit against both partners who guaranteed the lease. That suit was for approximately one hundred thousand dollars ($100,000); so the partners hired counsel to represent them in that matter and counsel filed an answer for both parties demanding a jury trial.

Knowing that a jury trial would take at least one year to get to trial, counsel began planning with both partners for their transfer of assets and a filing of bankruptcy one year and one day thereafter. It is important to understand at this point that a person may transfer assets to family members or family limited partnerships, but *one year* must be placed between the transfer and the filing of bankruptcy in order to keep it beyond the reach of the bankruptcy trustee.

Once both partners were properly positioned and waiting for the one year and one day between the transfers of property and the filing of their bankruptcy, counsel approached the attorney for the landlords and negotiated a settlement resulting in a payment to the landlord of approximately 7 cents on the dollar. This settlement enabled one of the partners to stay out of bankruptcy while the other continued to plan his.

Mr. A, the person who continued to plan his bankruptcy, had the equipment for the wine and cheese shop in a secured place for the Chapter 7 bankruptcy trustee assigned to the wine and cheese shop corporation case, and gave an inventory to the trustee advising of the location of the equipment. The trustee ultimately abandoned the equipment and, while Mr. A. was willing to have his corporation purchase equipment for ten cents on the dollar, obtained the equipment for free as a result of the trustee's unwillingness to go through the motions of a sale. It does not always happen this way, but on occasion the trustee will only go after assets where they believe there is sufficient value. If the trustee does not believe assets have sufficient value, they will abandon them, and those in possession will obtain their ownership.

Mr. A immediately transferred the assets to the corporation operated by his restaurant. Since this was another transfer, Mr. A was advised that he would have to put a year and a day between these transfers in order to keep that equipment out of the bankruptcy trustee's reach when he files his personal bankruptcy. During this period of one year, the landlord of Mr. A's restaurant made an offer to buy out the lease of the restaurant so that the landlord could convert it to a gas and go operation with a major oil company. Mr. A began to negotiate with the landlord through counsel and all agreed that the sublease holder, the corporate entity operating the restaurant, would be the recipient of any funds coming from the landlord because the restaurant would have to move its equipment to another location.

After a sufficient amount of time, one year and one day had passed from the last transfer, Mr. A filed for protection under Chapter 7 (liquidation) of the U.S. Bankruptcy Code in his name. Since the corporate entity operating the restaurant was not in bankruptcy, the equipment used by Mr. A to operate his restaurant was not at risk. In addition, the corporate stock owned by Mr. A for the operation of his restaurant had negative value because the lease obligation was much greater than the value of the equipment owned by the restaurant. Therefore, the stock held by Mr. A would not be at risk. Mr. A came through bankruptcy without losing control of any assets and could have been personally discharged from the lease on the restaurant, but he chose to assume the lease for the benefit of the restaurant.

The negotiations for the purchase of the lease by the landlord from the restaurant corporation were still in the negotiating stage, and any monies that would be paid for the lease by the landlord would go directly to the corporation owning the restaurant. That way the restaurant could be relocated to a better location and Mr. A could continue to earn a living for his family. The entire process took approximately eighteen (18) months.

Obviously long-term planning for Mr. A would have been much better, especially if he had planned his corporate entities in advance of actually operating the restaurant and wine and cheese shops. For the purposes of protecting corporate and personal assets, it is often best to create several corporations for the operation of one business. For example, it would be wise to have the corporation doing the business own absolutely nothing and holding all of the obligations while it leases equipment from another corporation owned by the same stockholders. A third corporation might control all of the accounts receivable. Therefore, in the event of a suit, all that a judgment creditor could get from the defendant corporation would be debt. That corporation could then declare bankruptcy, and liquidate all of the debt that is dischargeable while the equipment and accounts receivable would be available for the creation of another business using a similar, but legally different name. The new corporation would be debt free, but could still use a lot of the good will of the original corporation through the use of a similar name or similar trade name. Of course, the best time to do this would be at the beginning of the business rather than when creditors are knocking at the door.

HOW TO MAXIMIZE MARKETING DOLLARS!

1. Introduction: How to Maximize your Budget

It's the kind of challenge that can keep you up at night. As a small business owner, you need marketing to generate increased sales and income. But when sales and income are constrained, your marketing capacity is limited – just when you need that capacity most. The solution isn't as elusive as it seems: there are ways to market effectively on a budget, experts say. In fact, you can do it productively even when your company's budget doesn't include a line item for marketing.

Every piece of communication that you send out is a marketing opportunity. Make documents exciting that otherwise might be boring. Make them fun; put them to work. That includes your email signature line, which you can use to promote upcoming events, new products or services, or your social media pages.

2. Redefine Marketing and Reinvigorate Sales

Another productive strategy that costs you nothing more than a change in perspective. See, most people think about their marketing as getting new leads. Yet in marketing, the most expensive place to sell is to a new customer. To recapture business from old customers, contact them during down times and offer "a specific reason" for them to purchase from you again. And when you do pursue new leads, enlist the help of your best customers by soliciting referrals instead of relying passively on word of mouth.

Don't forget to solicit social media reviews. Endorsements from "real people" now carry more weight than traditional marketing messages. Whether you run a dry cleaner, an accounting firm, or a general contracting company, a customer who refers to you as "my" service provider is your best promoter, they say.

Some small business owners worry that soliciting reviews puts unwanted pressure on customers and can contain good relationships, but you don't have to word it in a way that says, "Leave me a good review". Just email those customers that you have a good relationship with, and ask for a review. That does amazing things for your SEO, as well, once you start racking up those good reviews.

3. Track Results for Repeat Success

What's the best marketing strategy for the budget you do have? The challenge I find with most small business owners is they have no real, reliable way that they track their marketing. To create your marketing roadmap, you need to know how to calculate your return on past marketing investments.

Let's say that last year, you invested $1,000 in a pay-per-click campaign that generated 100 leads. You also spent $10,000 to exhibit at a trade show that generated 1,000 leads. That means that with each marketing strategy, you spent $10 per lead. Now, that doesn't tell you how good the lead is, so you need the second number, which is your cost per sale. That will tell you how good the lead quality is. Your second step, then, is to look at how many of your leads from each marketing campaign resulted in a sale.

Once you have that number, you can compare the value of

the sale with the cost of the campaign. You can set up a simple spreadsheet to do all this, so the math is already pre-done. This is called your ROI per $1 invested.

This formula attaches a hard number to the value of a given marketing strategy and compares that number with the results produced by other strategies. Tracking those results helps you to project the most profitable use of your marketing budget going forward.

Your company's challenge will be greater if you're in startup mode or haven't tracked your past marketing performance. What's more, your mileage may vary from one year or even one quarter to another. But whatever your starting point, it's essential to collect and analyze each of these factors to develop a more predictable and profitable marketing strategy.

4.   Build your Budget and your Sales

Once you've decided what you can spend, how do you convert that raw number into a budget that will work as hard as it can for your business? Here is a six-step plan...

Step 1. Review your data, identify those with the highest ROI, and then determine which can be expanded. For example, if you've had huge success at a trade show, but it's the only one in your industry, then additional trade shows aren't an option.

Step 2. Once you've selected targets for expansion, record a results projection.

Step 3. Create a plan for tracking results going forward, and establish a schedule for reviewing those numbers to check them against your projections.

Step 4. Develop a marketing calendar, which is probably the

best internal control you have that ensures you don't screw up the dates. Start with hard dates, such as the trade show schedule or the date that a direct mailer must go out, and work backward from there to determine your internal deadlines.

Step 5. Pull the trigger and implement it.

Step 6. Review, at least once a quarter, how it went. Look at your scorecard to make adjustments going forward to optimize the use of your cash. And that's how you maximize your marketing dollars.

HOW TO BUILD A FACEBOOK PAGE FOR YOUE SMALL BUSINESS

Personal Facebook pages number in the millions and an increasing number of small business owners are establishing what Facebook calls "Fan Pages." You should start one for your small business because more than 5 million Facebook users a day become fans of various pages.

Here's how to do it:

1. **Create your personal page first.**

   To create a "business" (or "fan") page, log into your personal account – only logged in users can create a fan page – then go to the following URL: www.facebook.com/pages/create.php

2. **Determine what category your business falls into.**

   Brand? Product? Organization? Artist? Band? Public Figure? Pick the one that best fits your company.

3. **Create your business page.**

   Post photos, contact information, services, products, etc.

4. **Promote your business page.**

Post a link to it from your personal page. Buy social ads on Facebook directing users to your business page. And promote your Facebook business page using Twitter, Linked In, and your email newsletter to customers, your website and your blog.

Create a sub-domain of your Facebook business page (facebook.yourcompany.com) on your main domain that sends users to your Facebook business page.

Study Facebook ads and the specific demographics that will get buyers to your business page. For example, you can target various economic groups and geographical locations.

HOW TO DRIVE CUSTOMERS TO YOUR WEBSITE!

Four small tweaks can help you optimize your company's website. Even minor additions to your search engine optimization can significantly boost your website's viewership.

Here's how...

1. **Refine keywords:**

    The most common problem with small businesses tends to be misuse of metadata and descriptions. Use at least 300 to 400 words of original, high-quality content on the main page, and incorporate common search phrases on your website's main pages and your title tags, Meta descriptions and heading tags.

2. **Be geo-specific:**

    Include terms related to your geographical area of operation in your keywords.

3. **Complete site maps and robot files in your website's dashboard:**

    These Web tools help direct search engines to your website. Site maps are a list of pages that are accessible to search engine crawlers. Robot files prevent crawlers from reading certain pages of your website, allowing you to assign priority to the most important pages.

4. Get on Google+:

More search engines are picking up your social networking signals. Google is the most widely used search engine. Business owners can ensure they are getting maximum visibility by registering their business. Engage with other users to boost your ranking.

BEST ADVICE FROM 15 SELF-MADE MILLIONAIRES!

Rick Alden, founder of Skullcandy: "The fastest route to revenue wins." Coming up with ideas is never a problem for a creative team. Instead, the challenge is learning to say no to nine great ideas to free up the resources to push one product to market immediately. "The one product may not be your fantasy, but revenue on a simpler product today always beats running out of money developing a more complicated product that won't launch for another year."

Sheila Johnson, founder and CEO of Salamaner Hotels & Resorts: "Surround yourself with a great team, and build that team slowly. Your team is one of your most important investments, and if you are careful about hiring only the best people, it will pay dividends."

Peter Relan, founder of 9+: "It's all about the sailor." No matter how great an idea is, success in business is more about the sailor than the boat. "A great entrepreneur can take a bad idea and turn it into something incredible. This means that, while ideas are important, it's even more critical to have the right people in the right positions to execute them."

Melinda Emerson, founder and CEO of Quintessence Group: "Always know your next hire." There are countless

107

risks associated with being a small-business owner, and one of the biggest is staffing. "Nobody is going to love your business as much as you do, so you have to protect it." People will quit on the worst day possible – so long as it's advantageous for them. "Keep in touch with people you didn't hire but you really liked; you never know when you might need to call upon them to help you out."

Jim Murren, chairman and CEO of MGM Resorts International: "Spend most of your time looking forward." You need to have the capacity to envision the long term. "Creating teams that have an understanding of not only what they are doing but, why they are doing it, it critical."

Christine Day, CEO of Luvo: "If you wait for evidence, you'll be a follower, not a leader." You cannot rely on market research for innovation. "There is no evidence for what has not been created yet; only insight, purpose, passion and a willingness to move into what could be instead of what is. Truly innovative companies are not afraid to let go and create the next market shift."

Diane Bryant, senior vice president and GM of Data Center Group, Intel: "There is value in expanding and rounding out your expertise skill set." Just because you've been around the block doesn't mean you can't grow as a professional. "The better you understand your customer, the higher the probability of success." Learn firsthand what works and what doesn't.

Nick Lazaris, president and CEO of Corvan: "Trust yourself. In business, you have to act on your instincts because, ultimately, you will be the one who is responsible. If your decision fails, it ought to be something you really believed in. You want to be able to own up to it and learn from it."

Peter Thum, founder and CEO of Liberty United: "Choose to do the right thing. As an entrepreneur, you always will face adversity. You can't predict what that adversity will be, but if you try to do the right thing, and that right thing is based on a set of values you keep, ultimately you will come out well."

Shama Hyder, CEO and founder of Marketing Zen: "The first idea is rarely the best one." Ideas are like the people who have them – always changing, always getting better. "Most businesses start with what they think is a great idea, but in almost every case, the ideas change over time. In the past, business success used to be about having a bulletproof long-term strategy; now it's all about the ability to stay agile and adapt." The takeaway is simple: Constantly evaluate.

Josh Elman, partner of Greylock Partners: "Don't take calls – make calls. It's up to you to make things happen. So much of what happens in the world of business is inbound – you react to this, you field that. In reality, especially when you've decided to follow a passion, you should take matters into your own hands and push things outbound."

Khajak Keledjian, co-founder and chief executive of Intermix: "Focus on what makes you different. Creativity is to see what everyone else sees but think of what nobody else thought of. Focusing on that point of view, focusing on what makes you different, really is the most important way to stand out in the marketplace."

Rehan Choudhry, founder of Life is Beautiful: "Stop being scared, and jump. What makes an entrepreneur is not knowing everything about business, but rather being passionate and fearless. There's no 'right time' to take the leap; you can take it at any point in your life, and should." Don't overthink every decision or opportunity that comes your way. Stay focused and nimble.

Reece Pacheco, founder of Shelby.tv: "Be human." It's easy to focus on transactions, especially when you're struggling to start a company. But this is when it's most important to remember that your customers are people, too. "Take a second to recognize that there is a person on the other side of you. It can make all the difference in the world."

Kim Graham-Nye, co-founder and president of gDiapers: "Be sure to take care of yourself. We need to break the myth around 'balance' and create a new paradigm for understanding and valuing our time, our passions and our priorities in order to be our greatest selves."

BUSINESS RESOURCES

ACCOUNTING AND TAXES

American Accounting Association
(941) 921-7747
www.aaahq.org/index.cfin

American Institute of Certified Public Accountants
(212) 596-6200
www.aicpa.org

Association of Credit and Collection Professionals
(952) 926-6547
www.acainternational.org

CCH Inc.
(800) TELL-CCH
www.cch.com

Polaris International
International network of accounting firms
(305) 670-0580
www.accountants.org

INTERNET RESOURCES

Accounting Software Directory
www.cpaonline.com

American Express OPEN for Business resources,
Workshops, and articles related to small businesses, including financial management and marketing ideas
(800) 492-3344
wwwl33.americanexpress.co
mlosbnlLanding/informyourd
ecisions.asp

Checkfree
Offers different types of business payment solutions, including the option of paying bills and receiving payments electronically (678) 375-3000
www.checkfree.com

ADVERTISING AND MARKETING

American Advertising Federation
(202) 898-0089
www.aaf.org

American Marketing Association
(800) AMA-1150,
(312) 542-9000
www.ama.org

Direct Marketing Association
(212) 768-7277
www.the-dma.org

Marketing Research Association
(860) 682-1000
www.mra-net.org

Radio Advertising Bureau
(800) 232-3131
www.rab.com

INTERNET RESOURCES

ICANN (Internet Corp. for Assigned Names & Numbers)
Website domain name registration
(310) 823-9358
www.icann.org

Small Business Showcase
Small-business directory for advertising and marketing
(800) 706-6225
www.sbshow.com

Submit It!
Search engine optimization for small-business websites
Microsoft Corp.
(800) 642-7676

www.submit-it.com

24/7 Real Media Inc.
Provides marketing solutions and products
(212) 231-7100, (877) 247-2477
www.247realmedia.com

Website Marketing Plan
Lots of informative articles, as well as sample business and marketing plans
www.websitemarketingplan.com

CREDIT SERVICES

Dun & Bradstreet
Provides business credit-reporting services
(800) 234-3867
www.dnb.com

Equifax Credit Information Services Inc.
Provides credit-reporting services
(888) 202-4025
www.equifax.com

Experian
Provides credit-reporting services
(888) 397-3742
www.experian.com

First Data Merchant Services Corp.
Provides credit-processing services
(800) 735-3362, (303) 488-8000
www.firstdata.com

Telecheck
Provides check-guarantee services
(800) TELE-CHECK
www.telecheck.com

TransUnion
Provides credit-reporting services
(800) 888-4213
www.transunion.com

BUSINESS PLANNING AND DEVELOPMENT

INTERNET RESOURCES

BPlans.com
Free sample business plans, articles and online tools
(541) 683-6162
www.bplans.com

Business Plan Center
Sample business plans and planning guidelines for business owners

(800) 423-1228
http://businessplans.org

More Business
Sample business forms, agreements and marketing plans, as well as informative articles and links
http://morebusiness.com

Web Site 101
Free online tutorials, surveys and articles related to business planning
(562) 572-9702
http://website101.com

GENERAL BUSINESS RESOURCES

American Express OPEN for Business resources, workshops, and articles related to small businesses, including financial management and marketing ideas
(800) 492-3344
www.133.americanexpress.com/osbn/Landing/informyourdecisions.asp

American Management Association
(800) 262-9699,
(212) 586-8100

114

www.amanet.org

The Edward Lowe Foundation
(800) 232-LOWE
www.lowe.org

Equipment Leasing Association
(703) 527-8655
www.elaonline.com

Ewing Marion Kauffman Foundation
For entrepreneurship and education (816) 932-1000
www.kauffinan.org

Independent Insurance Agents & Brokers of America
(800) 221-7917
www.independentagent.com

Insurance Information Institute
Provides information and tools on how to adequately insure your business
(212) 346-5500
http://iii.org

National Association for Women's Business Owners

Resources and networking opportunities for women-owned businesses
(800) 55-NAWBO
www.nawbo.org

The National Association for the Self-Employed
(800) 232-6273
www.nase.org

National Association of Professional Employer Organizations
(703) 836-0466
www.napeo.org

National Minority Supplier Development Council
Certifies and matches minority-owned businesses with member corporations that want to purchase goods and services; its website also provides an exhaustive listing of relevant links
(212) 944-2430
www.nmsdc.org

Office Business Center Association International
Provides executive suite location assistance
(800) 237-4741, (614) 985-3633
www.officebusinesscenters.com

INTERNET RESOURCES

AOL Small Business
Tons of helpful articles for
every stage of your business
– from startup to managing to
growing your venture
http://smallbusiness.aol.com

BizBuySell
Useful website to find
businesses for sale, as well as
online tools and articles
(415) 284-4380
http://bizbuysell.com

Business Know-How
Ideas, advice, information
and resources for small and
homebased businesses
(631) 467-8883
http://businessknowhow.com

Business Owners Idea Café
Lots of ideas, articles and
resources to start and run a
business
www.businessownersideacafe.com

Business Town
Tons of resources and links to
start and run a small business
www.businesstown.com

**CCH Business Owner's
Toolkit**
Provides customizable
interactive forms and
spreadsheets, plus other
business tools and resources
www.toolkit.cch.com

Entrepreneur.com
Tons of resources, guides,
tips, articles and more at this
informative website for
startup businesses and
growing companies
(949) 261-2325
www.entrepreneur.com

The Entrepreneur Institute
provides resources and
networking opportunities for
business owners
(614) 895-1153
www.tei.net

Smart Biz
resources for small business,
including e-mail marketing
campaigns, creating a
website, and online tools and
equipment
www.smartbiz.com

TradePub.com
free trade publications and
white papers for small-
business owners

(800) 882-4670
www.tradepub.com

U.S. Business Advisor division of the SBA
www.business.gov
Yahoo! Small Business Resources news, articles, and resources on business basics, e-commerce, marketing, planning, accounting and more
http://smallbusiness.yahoo.com

HOMEBASED BUSINESS RESOURCES

American Home Business Association
(800) 664-2422
www.homebusiness.com

Mother's Home Business Network
(516) 997-7394
www.homeworkingmom.com

National Association of Home-Based Businesses
(410) 581-1373
www.usahomebusiness.com

INTERNET RESOURCE

Power Home Biz

lots of resources that include tools, articles and information on how to start, manage and grow a home business
http://powerhomebiz.com

INVENTORS AND IDEA PROTECTION

Affiliated Inventors Foundation Inc.
(719) 380-1234

American Society of Inventors
(215) 546-6601
www.americaninventor.org

Innovation Assessment Center Washington State University
(509) 335-6843
www.cbe.wsu.edu/-entrep/iac

Invention Services International
Sponsors the Invention Convention Trade Show Administrative & Communications Center
(800) 458-5624, (323) 460-4408
www.inventionconvention.com

The Inventors Assistance League International Inc.

(877) IDEA-BIN, (818) 246-6546 www.inventions.org

LAWS, REGULATIONS AND EMPLOYEE BENEFITS

INTERNET RESOURCES

Benefits Link
Informative website regarding employee benefits, laws and regulations
(407) 644-4146
http://benefitslink.com

BizFilings
Information on incorporating and related services for business owners, including forms, advice and tools needed
(800) 981-7183, (608) 827-5300 http://bizfilings.com

Employers of America
Information on writing job descriptions, HR manuals, safety tips, training resources and more; (800) 728-3187, (641) 424-3187
www.employerhelp.org

Find Law for Small Business

Links to regulatory agencies, sample forms and contracts, articles on all aspects of business development
(651) 687-7000
http://smallbusiness.findlaw.com

The Small Business Advisor
Lots of articles and advice for startup businesses
(703) 450 7049
www.isquare.com

Small Business Notes useful site that features a wide variety of business articles and resources, including legal issues and record-keeping
www.smallbusinessnotes.com

STARTUP ASSISTANCE

American Bankers Association
(800) BANKERS
www.aba.com

America's Community Bankers
(202) 857-3100
www.acbankers.org

Association of Small Business Development Centers
(703) 764-9850
www.asbdc-us.org

**Commercial Finance
Association**
(212) 594-3490
www.cfa.com

**Independent Community
Bankers of America**
(202) 659-8111
www.icba.org

**National Association of Small
Business Investment
Companies**
(202) 628-5055
www.nasbic.org

**National Business Incubation
Association**
Provides incubator location
assistance
(740) 593-4331
www.nbia.org

**National Venture Capital
Association**
(703) 524-2549
www.nvca.org

SCORE
National office (800) 634-0245
www.score.org

INTERNET RESOURCE

Business Finance
Thousands of business loan and
capital sources
(866) 892-9295
http://businessflnance.com

**GOVERNMENT
AGENCIES**

Copyright Clearance Center
222 Rosewood Dr.
(978) 750-8400
Danvers, MA 01923
info@copyright.com
www.copyright.com

Copyright Office
Library of Congress
101 Independence Ave. SE
Washington, DC 20559-6000
(202) 707-3000
www.loc.gov/copyright

Department of Agriculture
1400 Independence Ave. SW
Washington, DC 20250
(202) 720-7420
www.usda.gov
(202) 622-2000

Department of Commerce
1401 Constitution Ave. NW
Washington, DC 20230
(202) 482-2000
www.doc.gov

Department of Energy
1000 Independence Ave. SW
Washington, DC 20585

Department of the Interior
1849 C St. NI/V
Washington, DC 20240

Department of Labor
Frances Perkins Bldg.
200 Constitution Ave. NW
Washington, DC 20210
(866) 487-2365
www.dol.gov

Department of Treasury
Main Treasury Bldg.
1500 Pennsylvania Ave. NW
Washington, DC 20220
www.ustreas.gov

Export-Import Bank
of the United States
811 Vermont Ave. NW
Washington, DC 20571
(202) 565-3940
(800) 565-3946, ext. 3908
www.exim.gov

FCC
445 12th St. SW
Washington, DC 20544
(888) 225-5322
fccinfo@fcc.gov
www.fcc.gov

FTC
600 Pennsylvania Ave. NW
Washington, DC 20580
(202) 326-2222
www.ftc.gov

International Mail Calculator
http://ircalc.usps.gov

IRS
1111 Constitution Ave. NW
Washington, DC 20224
(202) 622-5000
www.irs.ustreas.gov

Minority Business Development Agency
U.S. Department of Commerce
1401 Constitution Ave. NW
Washington, DC 20230
(888) 324-1551
www.nbda.gov

Securities & Exchange Commission
100 F St. NE
Washington, DC 20549
(202) 551-6551
e-mail: help@sec.gov
www.sec.gov

Small Business Administration
409 Third St. SW
Washington, DC 20416

(800) 827-5722 www.sba.gov

**U.S. Consumer Product
Safety Commission Office of
Compliance**
4330 East-West Hwy.
Bethesda, MD 20814
(800) 638-2772
info@cpsc.gov
www.cpsc.gov

**U.S. Food and Drug
Administration**
5600 Fishers Ln.
Rockville, MD 20857
(888) 463-6332
www.fda.gov

**U.S. Patent & Trademark
Office**
P.O. Box 15667
Arlington, VA 22215
(800) 786-9199
www.uspto.gov

U.S. Printing Office
Superintendent of Documents
732 N. Capitol St. NW
Washington, DC 20401
(202) 512-0000
www.access.gpo.gov

SBA DISTRICT OFFICES
The SBA has several types of
field offices. The district

offices offer the fullest range of
services. To access all district
office websites, go to
www.sha.gov/regionslstates.html.

Alabama:
801 Tom Martin Dr., #201
Birmingham, AL 35211
(205) 290-7101

Alaska:
510LSt., #310
Anchorage, AK 99501-1952
(907) 271-4022

Arizona:
2828 N. Central Ave., #800
Phoenix, AZ 85004-1093
(602) 745-7200

Arkansas:
2120 Riverfront Dr., #250
Little Rock, AR 72202-1796
(501) 324-7379

California:
2719 N. Air Fresno Dr., #200
Fresno, CA 93727-1547
(559) 487-5791

330 N. Brand Blvd., #1200
Glendale, CA 91203-2304
(818) 552-3215

200W. Santa Ana Blvd., #700
Santa Ana, CA 92701-4134

(714) 550-7420

550W. C St., #550
San Diego, CA 92101
(619) 557-7250

455 Market St., 6th Fl.
San Francisco, CA 94105-2420

(415) 744-6820

650 Capitol Mall, #7-500
Sacramento, CA 95814-2413
(916) 930-3700

Colorado:
721 19th St., #426
Denver, CO 80202-2517
(303) 844-2607

Connecticut:
330 Main St., 2nd Fl.
Hartford, CT 06106-1800
(860) 240-4700

Delaware:
1007 N. Orange St., #1120
Wilmington, DE 19801-1232
(302) 573-6294

District of Columbia:
740 15th St. NW #300
Washington, DC 20005-3544
(202) 272-0345

Florida:

100 S. Biscayne Blvd., 7th Fl.
Miami, FL 33131-2011
(305) 536-5521

7825 Baymeadows WY,
#100-B
Jacksonville, FL 32256-7504
(904) 443-1900

Georgia:
233 Peachtree St. NE, #1900
Atlanta, GA 30303
(404) 331-0100

Hawaii:
300 Ala Moana Blvd., Rm. 2-
235; Box 50207
Honolulu, HI 96850-4981
(808) 541-2990

Idaho:
380 E. Parkcenter Blvd., #330
Boise, ID 83706
(208) 334-1696

Illinois:
500 W. Madison St., #1250
Chicago, IL 60661-2511
(312) 353-4528

3330 Ginger Creek Rd., Ste. B
Springfield, IL 62711
(217) 793-5020

Indiana:
8500 Keystone Crossing, #400

Indianapolis, IN 46240
(317) 226-7272

Iowa:
2750 First Ave. NE, #350
Cedar Rapids, IA 52402-4831
(319) 362-6405

210 Walnut St., Rm. 749
Des Moines, IA 50309-4106
(515) 284-4422

Kansas:
271 W. Third St. N., #2500
Wichita, KS 67202-1212
(316) 269-6616

Kentucky:
600 Dr. Martin Luther King Jr.
Pl.
Louisville, KY 40202
(502) 582-5971

Louisiana:
365 Canal St., #2820
New Orleans, LA 70130
(504) 589-6685

Maine:
Edward S. Muskie Federal Bldg.
68 Sewall St., Rm. 512
Augusta, ME 04330
(207) 622-8274

Maryland:

City Crescent Bldg.
10 S. Howard St., 6th Fl.
Baltimore, MD 21201-2525
(410) 962-4392

Massachusetts:
10 Causeway St., Rm. 265
Boston, MA 02222-1093
(617) 565-5590

Michigan:
McNamara Bldg.
477 Michigan Ave., #515
Detroit, MI 48226
(313) 226-6075

Minnesota:
Butler Square
210-C 100 N. Sixth St.
Minneapolis, MN 55403
(612) 370-2324

Mississippi:
AmSouth Bank Plaza
210 E. Capitol St., #900
Jackson, MS 39201
(601) 965-4378

Gulf Coast Business Technology
Center
1636 Popps Ferry Rd., #203
Biloxi, MS 39532
(228) 863-4449

New Mexico:

625 Silver Ave. SW, #320
Albuquerque, NM 87102
(505) 346-7909

Missouri:
323 W. Eighth St., #501
Kansas City; MO 64105 (816)
374-6701

200 N. Broadway, #1500
St. Louis, MO 63102
(314) 539-6600

Montana:
10 W. 15th St., #1100
Helena, MT 59626
(406) 441-1081

New York:
Niagara Center
130 S. Elmwood Ave., #540
Buffalo, NY 14202
(716) 551-4301

26 Federal Plaza, #3100
New York, NY 10278
(212) 264-4354

401 S. Salina St., 5th Fl.
Syracuse, NY 13202-2415
(315) 471-9393

Nebraska:
11145 Mill Valley Rd.
Omaha, NE 68154
(402) 221-4691

North Carolina:
6302 Fairview Rd., #300
Charlotte, NC 28210-2227
 (704) 344-6563

Nevada:
400 S. Fourth St., #250
Las Vegas, NV 89101
(701) 239-5131

North Dakota:
657 Second Ave. N., Rm. 219
Fargo, ND 58102
(702) 388-6611

New Hampshire:
JC Cleveland Federal Bldg.
55 Pleasant St., #3101
Concord, NH 03301
(603) 225-1400

New Jersey:
2 Gateway Center, 15th Fl.
Newark, NJ 07102
(973) 645-2434

Ohio:
1350 Euclid Ave., #211
Cleveland, OH 44115
(216) 522-4180

401 N. Front St., #200
Columbus, OH 43215
(614) 469-6860

Oklahoma:
Federal Bldg.
301 NW Sixth St.
Oklahoma City, OK 73102
(405) 609-8000

Oregon:
601 Second Ave. SW, #950
Portland, OR 97204-3192
(503) 326-2682

Pennsylvania:
Robert N.C. Nix Federal Bldg.
900 Market St., 5th Fl.
Philadelphia, PA 19107
(215) 580-2722

411 Seventh Ave., #1450
Pittsburgh, PA 15219
(412) 395-6560

Puerto Rico:
Citibank Tower
252 Ponce de Leon Ave., #200
San Juan, PR 00918
(787) 766-5572

Rhode Island:
380 Westminster St., Rm. 511
Providence, RE 02903
(401) 528-4561

Tennessee:
50 Vantage Wy., #201
Nashville, TN 37228-1500

(615) 736-5881

Texas:
4300 Amon Carter Blvd., #114
Ft. Worth, TX 76155
(817) 885-5500

8701 S. Gessner Dr., #1200
Houston, TX 77074
(713) 773-6500

222 E. Van Buren St., #500
Harlingen, TX 78550-6855
(956) 427-8533

1205 Texas Ave., Rm. 408
Lubbock, TX 79401-2693
(806) 472-7462

3649 Leopard St., #411
Corpus Christi, TX 78408
(361) 879-0017

10737 Gateway W.
El Paso, TX 79935
(915) 633-7001

17319 San Pedro, #200
San Antonio, TX 78232-1411
(210) 403-5900

South Carolina:
1835 Assembly St., Rm. 1425
Columbia, SC 29201
(803) 765-5377

South Dakota:
2329 N. Career Ave., #105
Sioux Falls, SD 57107
(605) 330-4243

U.S. Virgin Islands:
Sunny Isle Professional
Building Suites 5 & 6
St. Croix, US VI 00830
(340) 778-5380

Utah:
125 S. State St., Rm. 2227
Salt Lake City, UT
84138-1195
(801) 524-3209

310W. Wisconsin Ave.,
Rm. 400
Milwaukee, WI 53203
(414) 297-3941

Vermont:
87 State St., Rm. 205
Montpelier, VT 05601
(802) 828-4422

Virginia:
Federal Bldg.
400 N. Eighth St., #1150
Richmond, VA 23240-0126
(804) 771-2400

Washington:
2401 Fourth Ave., #450

Seattle, WA 98121
(206) 553-7310

801 W Riverside Ave., #200
Spokane, WA 99201
(509) 353-2811

West Virginia:
320 W. Pike St., #330
Clarksburg, WV 26301
(304) 623-5631

Wisconsin:
740 Regent St., #100
Madison, WI 53715
(608) 441-5263

Wyoming:
Federal Bldg.
100 E. B St.
P.O. Box 14001
Casper, WY 82602-5013
(307) 261-6500

**SMALL BUSINESS
DEVELOPMENT CENTERS**
The following SBDCs can
direct you to the lead SBDC in
your region. You can access all
SBDC websites at
www.sba.gov/sbdc and then
click on "SBDC Locator."

Alabama:
University of Alabama
2800 Milan Court, #124

Birmingham, AL 35211-6908
(205) 943-6750

Alaska:
University of Alaska,
Anchorage
430 W. Seventh Ave., #110
Anchorage, AK 99501
(907) 274-7232

Arizona:
Maricopa County Community
College
2411 W. 14th St., #132
Tempe, AZ 85281
(480) 731-8720

Arkansas:
University of Arkansas
2801 S. University Ave.
Little Rock, AR 72204
(501) 324-9043

California:
Santa Ana SBDC
(303) 892-3864
California State University
Fullerton
800 North State College Bl.,
LH640
Fullerton, CA 92834
(714) 278-2719

Fresno SBDC

University of California,
Merced
550 East Shaw, #105A
Fresno, CA 93710
(559) 241-6590

Los Angeles Region SBDC
Long Beach Community
College District
3950 Paramount BLV, #101
Lakewood, CA 90712
(562) 938-5004

Sacramento SBDC
California State University,
Chico
Chico, CA 95929-0765
(530) 898-4598

San Francisco SBDC
Humboldt State University
Office of Economic
Development
1 Harpst St., 2006A, Siemens
Hall
Arcata, CA 95521
(707) 826-3922

San Diego SBDC
Southwestern Community
College District
900 Otey Lakes Rd.
Chula Vista, CA 91910
(619)482-6388

Colorado:
Office of Economic
Development
1625 Broadway, #170
Denver, CO 80202

Connecticut:
University of Connecticut
1376 Storrs Road, Unit 4094
Storrs, CT 06269-1094
(860) 870-6370

Delaware:
Delaware Technology Park
1 Innovation Wy., #301
Newark, DE 19711
(302) 831-2747

District of Columbia:
Howard University School of
Business
2600 Sixth St. NW, Rm. 128
Washington, DC 20059
(202) 806-1550

Florida:
University of West Florida
401 E. Chase St., #100
Pensacola, FL 32502
(850) 473-7800

Georgia:
University of Georgia
Chicopee Complex
1180 E. Broad St.
Athens, GA 30602-5412

(706) 542-6762

Guam:
University of Guam
P.O. Box 5014, UOG Station
Mangilao, Guam 96923
(671) 735-2590

Hawaii:
University of Hawaii - Hilo
308 Kamehameha Ave., #201
Hilo, HI 96720
(808) 974-7515

Idaho:
Boise State University
1910 University Dr.
Boise, ID 83725-1655
(208) 426-3799

Illinois:
Department of
Commerce
and Economic Opportunity
620 E. Adams, S-4
Springfield, IL 62701
(217) 524-5700

Indiana:
Indiana Economic
Development Corp.
One North Capitol, #900
Indianapolis, IN 46204
(317) 234-8872

Iowa:
Iowa State University
340 Gerdin Business Bldg.
Ames, IA 50011-1350
(515) 294-2037

Kansas:
214 SW Sixth St., #301
Topeka, KS 66603
(785) 296-6514

Kentucky:
University of Kentucky
225 Garton College of Business
Lexington, KY 40506-0034
(859) 257-7668

Louisiana:
University of Louisiana –
Monroe
College of Business
Administration
700 University Ave.
Monroe, LA 71209-6530
(318) 342-5506

Maine:
University of Southern Maine
96 Falmouth St.
P.O. Box 9300
Portland, ME 04104-9300
(207) 780-4420

Maryland:
University of Maryland

7100 Baltimore Ave., #401
College Park, MD 20742
(301) 403-8300

Massachusetts:
University of Massachusetts
School of Management,
Rm. 205
Amherst, MA 01003-4935
(413) 545-6301

Michigan:
Grand Valley State University
Fort Hays State University
510 W. Fulton St.
Grand Rapids, MI 49504
(616) 331-7485

Minnesota:
Minnesota Small Business
Development Center
1st National Bank Bldg.
332 Minnesota St., Ste. E200
St. Paul, MN 55101-1351
(651) 297-5773

New Hampshire:
108 McConnell Hall
University of New Hampshire
Durham, NH 03824-3593
(603) 862-4879

New Jersey:
Rutgers University
49 Bleeker St.

Newark, NJ 07102-1993
(973) 353-5950

Mississippi:
University of Mississippi
P.O. Box 1848
B 19 Jeanette Phillips Dr.
University, MS 38677-1848
(662) 915-5001

Missouri:
University of Missouri
1205 University Ave., #300
Columbia, MO 65211
(573) 882-1348

Montana:
Department of Commerce
301 S. Park, Rm.114
P.O. Box 200501
Helena, MT 59620
(406) 841-2746

Nebraska:
University of Nebraska -
Omaha
60th & Dodge Sts.,
CBA Rm. 407
Omaha, NE 68182
(402) 554-2521

Nevada:
Bismarck,
University of Nevada –
Reno
CBA, Rm. 411

Reno, NV 89557-0100
(775) 784-1717

New Mexico:
Santa Fe Community College
Lead Center
6401 S. Richards Ave.
Santa Fe, NM 87508
(505) 428-1362

New York:
State University of New York
SUNY Plaza, S-523
Albany, NY 12246
(518) 443-5398

North Carolina:
University of North Carolina
5 W. Hargett St., #600
Raleigh, NC 27601-1348
(919) 715-7272

North Dakota:
University of North Dakota
1600 E. Century Ave., #2
ND 58503
(701) 328-5375

Ohio:
Ohio Department of
Development
77 S. High St.
Columbus, OH 43216
(614) 466-5102

Oklahoma:

130

Southeastern Oklahoma State
University 517 W.
University Blvd.,
Box 2584, Sm. A
Durant, OK 74701
(580) 745-7577

Oregon:
Lane Community College 99W.
l0thAve., #390
Eugene, OR 97401-3021
(541) 463-5250

Pennsylvania:
University of Pennsylvania
The Wharton School
3733 Spruce St. Philadelphia, PA
19104-6374
(215) 898-1219

Puerto Rico:
Inter-American University of
Puerto Rico
416 Ponce de Leon Ave.
Union Plaza, 7th Fl.
Hato Rey, PR 00918
(787) 763-6811

Rhode Island:
Bryant University
1150 Douglas Pike
Smithfield, RI 02917
(401) 232-6923

South Carolina:

University of South Carolina
College of Business
Administration
1710 College St.
Columbia, SC 29208
(803) 777-4907

South Dakota:
University of South Dakota
Patterson Hall 414 E. Clark St.
Vermillion, SD 57069-2390
(605) 677-6256

Tennessee:
Tennessee Board of Regents
1415 Murfressboro Rd., #540
Nashville, TN 37217-2833
(615) 898-2745

Texas:
Houston SBDC
University of Houston 2302
Fannin, #200
Houston, TX 77002
(713) 752-8425

North SBDC
Dallas County Community
College 1402 Corinth St.
Dallas, TX 75215
(214) 860-5835

NW SBDC
Texas Tech University

2579 South Loop 289, #114
Lubbock, TX 79423
(806) 745-3973

Southwest Texas Border
Region SBDC
University of Texas, San
Antonio
501 West Durango Bl.
San Antonio, TX 78207-4415
(210) 458-2742

Utah:
Salt Lake Community College
9750 S. 300W. Sandy, UT
84070
(801) 957-3493

Vermont:
Vermont Technical College
P.O. Box 188, 1 Main St.
Randolph Center, VT 05061-0188
(802) 728-9101

Virginia:
George Mason University
4031 University Dr. #200
Fairfax, VA 22030-3409
(703) 277-7727

Washington:
Washington State University
534 E. Trent Ave.
P.O. Box 1495
Spokane, WA 99210-1495

(509) 358-7765

West Virginia:
West Virginia Development
Office Capital Complex
Bldg. 6, Rm. 652
Charleston, WV 25301
(304) 558-2960

Wisconsin:
University of Wisconsin
432 North Lake St., Rm. 423
Madison, WI 53706
(608) 263-7794

Wyoming:
University of Wyoming
P.O. Box 3922
Laramie, WY 82071-3922
(307) 766-3505

**STATE COMMERCE &
ECONOMIC
DEVELOPMENT
DEPARTMENTS**

Alabama:
(800) 248-0033,
(334) 242-0400
www.ado.state.aLus

Alaska:
(907) 465-2500
www.dced.state.ak.us

Arizona:

(602) 771-1100
www.state.az.us

Arkansas:
(800) ARKANSAS,
(501) 682-1121
www.1-800-arkansas.com

California:
(916) 324-9538
www.commerce.ca.gov

Colorado:
(303) 892-3840
www.state.co.us/oed/edc

Connecticut:
(860) 571-7136
www.cerc.com

Delaware:
(302) 739-4271
www.state.de.us/dedo

District of Columbia:
(202) 727-1000
www.dc.gov/agencies/index.asp

Louisiana:
(800) 450-8115,
(225) 342-3000
www.lded.state.la.us

Florida:
(407) 316-4600
www.eflorida.com

Maine:
(207) 624-9800
www.econdevmaine.com

Georgia:
(404) 679-4940
www.dca.state.ga.us

Maryland:
(410) 704-3776
www.choosemaryland.org

Hawaii:
(808) 586-2423
www.hawaii.gov/dbedt

Massachusetts:
(877) 249-8326
www.state.ma.us/mobd

Idaho:
(800) 842-5858,
(208) 334-2470
www.idoc.state.id.us

Michigan:
(517) 373-9808
www.michigan.gov

Illinois:
(312) 814-7179
www.commerce.state.il.us

Minnesota:

(800) 657-3858,
(651) 297-1291
www.deed.state.mn.us

Indiana:
(317) 232-8800
www.state.in.us/doc

Mississippi:
(601) 359-3449
www.mississippi.org

Iowa:
(515) 242-4700
www.iowalifechanging.comlbusiness

Missouri:
(573) 751-4962
www.ded.mo.gov

Kansas:
(785) 296-3481
http://kdoch.state.ks.us/public

Montana:
(406) 841-2700
www.commerce.state.mt.us

Kentucky:
(800) 626-2930,
(502) 564-7140
www.thinkkentucky.com

Nebraska:
(800) 426-6505
www.neded.org

Nevada:
(702) 486-2750
www.dbi.state.nv.us

Pennsylvania:
(866) 466-3972
www.inventpa.com

New Hampshire:
(603) 271-2411
www.dred.state.nh.us

Rhode Island:
(401) 222-2601
www.riedc.com

New Jersey:
(609) 777-0885
vAv-w.state.nj.us/commerce

South Carolina:
(803) 777-5118
www.myscgov.com

New Mexico:
(800) 374-3061, (505) 827-
0300
www.edd.state.nm.us

South Dakota:
(800) 872-6190, (605) 773-
3301
www.sdreadytowork.com

New York:

(800) 782-8369
www.empire.state.ny.us

Tennessee:
(615) 741-2626
www.state.tn.us/ecdlcon_bsv.htm

North Carolina:
(800) 258-0862,
(919) 715-7272
www.sbtdc.org

Texas:
(512) 463-2000
www.governor.state.tx.us/divis
ions/ecodev/sba

North Dakota:
(701) 777-3132
www.innovators.net

Utah:
(801) 538-8770
http://goed.utah.gov

Ohio:
(614) 466-4232
www.odod.state.oh.us/onestop

Vermont:
(802) 828-3211
www.state.vt.us/dca

(Commerce and Community
Development Agency)
www.thinkvermont.com

(Economic Development
Agency)

Oklahoma:
(800) 879-6552
www.okcommerce.gov

Oregon:
(503) 986-0123
www.econ.state.or.us

Virginia:
(804) 371-8200
www.dba.state.va.us
www.dba.state.va.us/smdev

Wisconsin:
(608) 266-1018
www.commerce.state.wi.us

Washington:
(360) 725-4100
www.cted.wa.gov

Wyoming:
(800) 262-3425,
(307) 777-2800
www.wyomingbusiness.org

West Virginia:
(304) 558-2234
www.wvdo.org

**SMALL-BUSINESS
FRIENDLY BANKS**

Following is a listing of the SBA's top small-business-friendly banks in each state.

ALABAMA

Camden National Bank
Camden, AL
(3 34) 682-4215
www.camdennationalbank.net

Citizens Bank of Fayette
 Fayette, AL
(205) 932-4226

Community Bank
Blountsville, AL
(205) 429-1000
www.cbblount.com

Farmers & Merchants
Bank Piedmont, AL
(256) 447-9041
www.f-mbank.com

First Citizens Bank
Luverne, AL
(334) 335-3346
www.fcbl.com

First National Bank of Central
Alabama
Aliceville, AL
(205) 373-2922
www.fnbca.com

First National Bank of Talladega
Talladega, AL
(256) 362-2334
www.fnbtalladega.com

Merchants Bank
Jackson, AL
(251) 246-4425
www.merchantsbank.com

Peachtree Bank
Maplesville, AL
(334) 366-2921

Peoples Bank of Coffee County
Elba, AL
(334) 897-2252

Peoples Southern Bank
Clanton, AL
(205) 755-7691
www.peoplessouthern.com

Small Town Bank
Wedowee, AL
 (256) 357-4936
www.smalltownbank.com

Traders & Farmers Bank
Haleyville, AL
(205) 486-5263

ALASKA

First Bank
Ketchikan, AK (907) 228-4226

www.firstbankak.com

ARIZONA

Meridian Bank (formerly
Community Bank of Arizona)
Wickenburg, AZ
(92 8) 684-7884
www.meridianbank.com

Stockmen's Bank
Kingman, AZ
(928) 757-7171
www.stockmensbank.com

Sunstate Bank
Casa Grande, AZ
(520) 836-4666
 www.sunstatebank.com

Western Security Bank
Scottsdale, AZ
(480) 367-9494

ARKANSAS

Arvest Bank-Yellville
(Formerly Bank of Yellville)
Yellville, AR
(870) 449-4231
www.bankofyellville.com

Bank of Pocahontas
Pocahontas, AR
(870) 892-5286

Bank of Salem
Salem, AR
(870) 895-2591

Commercial Bank & Trust
Monticello, AR
(870) 367-6221
www.commercial-bank.net

Community Bank
Cabot, AR
(501) 843-3575
www.communitybk.net

DeWitt Bank & Trust
DeWitt, AR
(870) 946-8089
www.dewittbank.com

First National Bank
Hot Springs, AR
(501) 525-7999
www.fnbhotsprings.com

First National Bank of Sharp
County
Ash Flat, AR
(870) 994-2311
www.fnbsharpcounty.com

First Service Bank
Greenbrier, AR
(501) 679-7300
www.firstservice.com

Malvern National Bank
Malvern, AR
(501) 332-6955

Pinebluff National Bank
Pinebluff, AR
(870) 535-7222

Southern State Bank
www.pacificwesternbank.com
Malvern, AR
(501) 332-2462

CALIFORNIA

Bank of the Sierra
Porterville, CA
(559) 782-4900
www.bankofthesierra.com

California Center Bank
Los Angeles, CA
(213) 386-2222
www.centerbank.com

Community Commerce Bank
Los Angeles, CA
www.ccombank.com
(323) 268-6100

Cupertino National Bank
Cupertino, CA
(408) 725-4400
www.cupnb.com

Inland Community Bank
Rialto, CA
(909) 874-4444
www.icbbank.com

Nara Bank
www.mnbbank.com
Los Angeles, CA
(213) 639-1700
www.narabankna.com

Pacific Western Bank
www.pbnb.net
Santa Monica, CA
(310) 458-1521

Plumas Bank
www.southernstatebank.com
Quincy CA
(530) 283-6800
www.plumasbank.com

San Joaquin Bank
Bakersfield, CA
(661) 281-0300
www.sjbank.com

Valley Independent Bank
El Centro, CA
 (760) 337-3200
www.vibank.com

Wells Fargo Bank
San Francisco, CA
(415) 437-1582
www.wellsfargo.com

Wilshire State Bank
Los Angeles, CA
(213) 387-3200
www.wilshirebank.com

COLORADO

Canon National Bank
Canon City, CO
(719) 276-9153
www.canonbank.com

Pine River Valley Bank
Bayfield, CO
(970) 884-9583

Centennial Bank
Pueblo, CO
(719) 543-0763

Wells Fargo
(Formerly Bank of Grand
Junction)
Grand Junction, CO
www.coloradosbank.com

(970) 241-9000
www.wellsfargo.com

Cheyenne Mountain Bank
Colorado Springs, CO
(719) 579-9150
www.cmbank.com

Colonial Bank
Aurora, CO
(505) 671-9000
www.colonialbk.com

Farmers State Bank of Caihan
Calhan, CO
(719) 347-2727
www.farmers-statebank.com

First Community Bank
(formerly First
Community Industrial Bank)
Denver, CO
(303) 399-3400
www.fsbnm.com

First National Bank of Las
Animas
Las Animas, CO
(719) 456-1512

Park State Bank and Trust
Woodland Park, CO
(719) 687-9234
www.psbtrust.com

CONNECTICUT

Castle Bank and Trust
Meriden, CT
(203) 639-8866
www.castlebankandtrust.com

Citizens National Bank

Putnam, CT
(860) 928-7921
www.cnbct.com

Cornerstone Bank
Stamford, CT
(203) 356-0111
www.cornerstonebank.com

Salisbury Bank & Trust
Company
Lakeville, CT
(860) 435-9801
www.salisbury-bank.com

DELAWARE

Bank of Delmarva
Seaford, DE
(302) 629-2700
www.bankofdelmarva.com

Bank One (formerly First USA
Bank)
Wilmington, DE
(302) 594-4000
www.bankone.com

Citibank Delaware
New Castle, DE
(302) 323-3900
www.citicorp.com

DISTRICT OF COLUMBIA

Adams National Bank

Washington, DC
(202) 772-3600
www.adamsbank.com

FLORIDA

Apalachicola State Bank
(850) 653-8805
Apalachicola, FL
www.apalachicolastatebank.com

Citrus & Chemical Bank
Bartow, FL
(863) 533-3171
www.candcbank.com

Columbia County Bank
Lake City, FL
(386) 752-5646

Drummond Community Bank
Chiefland, FL
(352) 493-2277

Destin Bank
Destin, FL
(850) 837-8100
www.destlnbank.com

First National Bank of Alachua
Alachua, FL
(386) 462-1041
www.fnba.net

First National Bank of
Wauchula

Wauchula, FL
(863) 773-4136

Independent National Bank
Ocala, FL
(352) 854-4004
ww.inatbank.com

Suntrust Bankcard
Orlando, FL
(407) 237-4203
www.suntrust.com

Transatlantic Bank
Coral Gables, FL
(305) 666-0200
www.transatlanticbank.com

GEORGIA

Bank of Dudley
www.ccbanc.com
Dudley, GA
(478) 676-3196
www.bankofdudley.com

Capitol City Bank & Trust
Atlanta, GA
(404) 752-6067
www.capitolcitybank-atl.com

Citizens Bank of Washington
County
Sandersville, GA
(478) 552-5116

www.cbwc.com

First Bank & Trust
Carnesville, GA
(706) 384-4546
www.firstbankandtrust-ga.com

Community National Bank
Ashburn, GA
(229) 567-9686
www.communitynational-
bank.com

Community Banking
Company of Fitzgerald
Fitzgerald, GA
(229) 423-4321

Farmers & Merchants Bank
Lakeland, GA
(229) 482-3585
www.fmbnk.com

First Bank of Coastal Georgia
Pembroke, GA
(912) 653-4396
www.firstbankofcg.com
First State Bank
Stockbridge, GA
(770) 474-7293
www.firststateonline.com

McIntosh State Bank
Jackson, GA
(770) 775-8300

www.mcintoshbancshares.com

Planters First Bank
Cordele, GA
 (229) 273-2416
www.plantersfirst.com

Sunmark Community Bank
Hawkinsville, GA
(478) 783-4036
www.sunmarkbank.com

The United Banking Company,
Nashville, GA
(229) 686-9451

HAWAII

First Hawaiian Bank
Honolulu, HI
(808) 525-7000
www.fhb.com

IDAHO

Mountain West Bank
(Formerly Pend Oreille Bank)
Sandpoint, ID
(208) 265-2232
www.mountainwest-bank.com

ILLINOIS

Anna National Bank
Anna, IL
(618) 833-8506

www.annanational.com

Bank of Pontiac
Pontiac, IL
(815) 842-1069
www.bankofpontiac.com

First National Bank-Employee
Owned Antioch, IL
(847) 838-2265
www.fnbeo.com

First National Bank in Toledo
Toledo, IL
(217) 849-2701
wwrw.firstneighbor.com

First National Bank of Ottawa
Ottawa, IL
(815) 434-0044
www.firstottawa.com

Germantown Trust & Savings
Bank
Breese, IL
(618) 526-4202
www.gtsb.com

National Bank of Petersburg
Petersburg, IL
(217) 632-3241

Peoples National Bank of
Kewanee
Kewanee, IL
(309) 853-3333

142

www.pnb-kewanee.com

Peotone Bank and Trust
Peotone, IL
(708) 258-3231
www.peotonebank.com

Trustbank
Olney, IL
(618) 395-4311
www.trustbank.net

INDIANA

Campbell & Fetter Bank
Kendallville, IN
(260) 343-3300
www.campbellfetterbank.com

DeMotte State Bank
DeMotte, IN
(219) 987-4141
www.netdsb.com

First Farmers Bank & Trust
Converse, IN
(765) 395-7746
www.ffbt.com

First Harrison Bank (formerly
Hometown National Bank)
New Albany, IN
(812) 949-2265
www.firstharrisonbank.com

First National Bank of
Monterey
Monterey, IN
(574) 542-2121
www.pwrte.coml-monterey

First State Bank
Brazil, IN
(812) 448-3357
www.first-online.com

First State Bank of Middlebury
Middlebury, IN
(574) 825-2166
www.fsbmiddlebury.com

Fowler State Bank
Fowler, IN
(765) 884-1200

Heritage Community Bank
Columbus, IN
(765) 485-5175
www.heritagecb.com

Markle Bank
Markle, IN
(260) 375-4550
www.marklebank.com

Scott County State Bank
Scottsburg, IN
(812) 752-4501
www.scottcountystatebank.com

State Bank of Oxford

Oxford, IN
(765) 385-2213
www.statebankofoxford.com

IOWA

Farmers State Bank
Jesup, IA
(319) 827-1050
www.fsb1879.com

First State Bank of Colfax
Colfax, IA
(515) 674-3533

Freedom Security Bank
Coralville, IA
(319) 688-9005
www.fs-bank.com

Houghton State Bank
Red Oak, IA
(712) 623-4823
www.houghtonstatebank.com

Bank Iowa
Red Oak, IA
(712) 623-6960
www.bankredoak.com

Lee County Bank & Trust Co.
Fort Madison, IA
 (319) 372-2243
www.lcbtrust.com

Community First Bank

Keosauqua, IA
(319) 293-6283
www.cfirst.com

Libertyville Savings Bank
Fairfield, IA
(641) 693-3141
www.libertyvillesavingsbarik.com

Cresco Union Savings Bank
Cresco, IA
(563) 547-2040
www.cusb.com

Maquoketa State Bank
Maquoketa, IA
(563) 652-2491
www.maquoketasb.com

Decorah Bank & Trust
Decorah, IA
(563) 382-9661
www.securitybank-decorah.com

Northstar Bank
Estherville, IA
(712) 362-3322
www.northstarbankiowa.com

Security State Bank
Red Oak, IA
(712) 623-9809
www.securitystatebank.net

144

KANSAS

Gardner National Bank
Gardner, KS
(913) 856-7199
www.gardnernational.com

Peoples Bank & Trust
McPherson, KS
(620) 241-2100
www.peoplesbankonline.com

Citizens State Bank
Gridley, KS
 (620) 836-2888

Rose Hill Bank
Rose Hill, KS
(316) 776-2131
www.rosehillbank.com

Emporia State Bank & Trust
Emporia, KS
(620) 342-8655
www.ebtrust.com

Union State Bank
Everest, KS
(785) 548-7521

Farmers State Bank of
McPherson
McPherson, KS
(620) 241-3090

First National Bank
Hays, KS
(785) 628-2400
www.bankhays.com

First National Bank of
Southern Kansas
Mount Hope, KS
(316) 661-2471

First State Bank
Norton, KS
(785) 877-3341
www.firstatebank.com

University National Bank
Pittsburg, KS
(620) 231-4200

First National Bank
Independence, KS
 (620) 331-2265
www.bankindependence.com

KENTUCKY

Bank of Columbia
Columbia, KY
(270) 384-6433
www.bankcolumbia.com

Bank of Edmonson County
Brownsville, KY
(270) 597-2175
www.bankofedmonson.com

Citizens Bank
Mount Vernon, KY
(606) 256-2500

Farmers Bank, The
Hardinsburg, KY
(270) 756-2166
www.thefarmersbank-ky.com

Farmers National Bank of
Danville
Danville, KY
(859) 236-2926
www.farmnatldan.com

First National Bank of
Columbia
Columbia, KY
(270) 384-2361

Kentucky Banking Centers
Glasgow, KY
(270) 651-2265
www.kbc123.com

Peoples Bank of Fleming
County
Flemingsburg, KY
(606) 845-2461
www.pbfco.com

Peoples Bank & Trust
Company of Hazard
Hazard, KY
(606) 436-2161
www.peopleshazard.com

South Central Bank
Glasgow, KY
(270) 651-7466
www.southcentralbank.biz

LOUISIANA

American Bank
Welsh, LA
(337) 734-2226

City Savings Bank and Trust
Co.
DeRidder, LA
(337) 463-8661
www.citysavingsbank.com

Community Bank
Mansfield, LA
(318) 872-3831
www.cbexpress.com

Delta Bank
(318) 336-4510
Vidalia, LA
www.fnbcolumbia.com

Feliciana Bank & Trust Co.
Clinton, LA
(225) 344-8890

First Louisiana National Bank
Breaux Bridge, LA
(337) 332-5960

146

Gibsland Bank & Trust Co.
Gibsland, LA
(318) 843-6228
www.gibslandbank.com

Guaranty Bank
Mamou, LA
(337) 468-5274

Gulf Coast Bank
Abbeville, LA
 (337) 893-7733
www.gcbank.com

Jeff Davis Bank & Trust
Jennings, LA
(337) 824-3424
www.jdbank.com

MAINE

First Citizens Bank
Presque Isle, ME
(207) 768-3222
www.fcbmaine.com

MARYLAND

Bank of the Eastern Shore
Cambridge, MD
(410) 228-5800
www.bankofes.com

Farmers & Mechanics Bank
Frederick, MD

(301) 644-4400
www.fmbancorp.com

First United Bank and Trust
Co.
Oakland, MD
(888) 692-2654
www.myfirstunited.com
Hebron Savings Bank
Hebron, MD
(410) 749-1185
www.hebronsavingsbank.com

Patapsco Bank
Dundalk, MD
(410) 285-1010
www.patapscobank.com

Peninsula Bank
Princess Anne, MD
 (410) 651-2404
www.peninsulabankmd.com

Peoples Bank of Kent County
Chestertown, MD
(410) 778-3500
www.pbkc.com

Talbot Bank of Easton
Easton, MD
(410) 822-1400
www.talbot-bank.com

MASSACHUSETTS

Bank of Western
Massachusetts
Springfield, MA
(413) 781-2265
www.bankwmass.com

Capital Crossing Bank
Boston, MA
(617) 880-1050
www.capitalcrossing.com

Enterprise Bank & Trust
Company
Lowell, MA
(978) 459-9000
www.ebtc.com

Horizon Bank & Trust
Company
Braintree, MA
(781) 794-9992
www.bankhorizon.com

Westbank
West Springfield, MA
(413) 747-1432
www.westbankonline.com

MICHIGAN

Century Bank & Trust
Goldwater, MI
(517) 278-1500
www.centurybt.com

First National Bank & Trust
Co. of Iron Mountain
Iron Mountain, MI
(906) 774-2200
www.fnbimk.com

First National Bank of America
East Lansing, MI
(517) 351-2665
www.fnba.com

Firstbank
Mount Pleasant, MI
(989) 773-2600
www.firstbank-mtp.com

Firstbank-Alma
Alma, MI
(989) 463-3131
www.firstbank-mtp.com

Firstbank-West Branch
West Branch, MI
(989) 345-7900
www.firstbank-mtp.com

Hillsdale County National
Bank
Hillsdale, MI
(517) 439-4300
www.countynationalbank.com

Michigan Heritage Bank
Farmington, MI
(248) 538-2545
www.miheritage.com

Peninsula Bank of Ishpeming
Ishpeming, MI
(906) 485-6333
www.penbank.com

Peoples State Bank of
Munising
Munising, MI
(906) 387-2006
www.bankatpsb.com

State Bank of Caledonia
Caledonia, MI
(616) 891-8113
www.sbcal.org

MINNESOTA

Boundary Waters Community
Bank
Ely, MN
(218) 365-6181
www.bwcb.com

First Independent Bank
Russell, MN
(507) 532-2426

First National Bank
Bagley, MN
(218) 694-6233
www.fnbbagley.com

First State Bank Alexandria-
Carlos
Alexandria, MN
(320) 763-7700
www.fsbalex.com

First State Bank of Le Center
Le Center, MN
(507) 357-2225

Heritage Bank
Willmar, MN
(320) 235-5722
www.heritagebankna.com

Kasson State Bank
Kasson, MN
(507) 634-7022

Northland Community Bank
Northome, MN
(218) 897-5285

Peoples National Bank of Mora
Mora, MN
(320) 679-3100
www.pnbmora.com

Pine River State Bank
Pine River, MN
(218) 587-4463
www.pineriverstatebank.com/
pineriveroffice.html

Washington County Bank

Oakdale, MN
 (651) 702-3976
www.wcbanknet

MISSISSIPPI

Bank of New Albany
New Albany, MS
(662) 534-9511
www.bankofnewalbany.com

Bank of Holly Springs
Holly Springs, MS
(662) 252-2511
www.bankoffiollysprings.com

Farmers & Merchants Bank
Baldwyn, MS
 (662) 365-1200
www.fmbms.com

First National Bank of
Pontotoc
Pontotoc, MS
(662) 489-1631
www.kassonstatebank.com

First State Bank
Holly Springs, MS
(662) 252-4211

Mechanics Bank
Water Valley, MS
(662) 473-2261
www.mechanicsbankms.com

Merchants & Marine Bank
Pascagoula, MS
 (228) 934-1323
www.mandmbank.com

Omnibank
Mantee, MS
(662) 456-5341

Pike County National Bank
McComb, MS
(601) 684-7575

MISSOURI

Callaway Bank
Fulton, MO
(573) 642-3322
www.callawaybank.com

Century Bank of the Ozarks
Gainesville, MO
(417) 679-3321
www.cbozarks.com

Community State Bank
Bowling Green, MO
(573) 324-2233
www.c-s-b.com

First Missouri State Bank
Poplar Bluff, MO
(573) 785-6800
www.firstmissouristatebank.net

First National Bank

Mountain View, MO
(417) 934-2033 www.fnb-
fnb.com

Kearney Trust Company
Kearney, MO
(816) 628-6666
www.kearneytrust.com

Mid-Missouri Bank
Springfield, MO
(417) 877-9191
www.mid-missouribank.com

O'Bannon Bank
Buffalo, MO
(417) 345-6207
www.obannonbank.com

Palmyra State Bank
Palmyra, MO
(573) 769-2001
www.palmyrastatebank.net

Peoples Bank
Cuba, MO
(573) 885-2511
www.peoplesbk.com

Perry State Bank
Perry, MO
(573) 565-2221
www.perrystatebk.com

Security Bank of Southwest
Missouri
Cassville, MO
(417) 847-4794
Southwest Missouri Bank

Carthage, MO
(417)358-9331
www.smbonline.com

Town & Country Bank
Salem, MO
(573) 729-6157
www.tcbanks.com

MONTANA

Citizens State Bank
Hamilton, MT
 (406) 363-3551
www.citizensstbank.com

First Citizens Bank of Butte
Butte, MT
(406) 494-4400

First Community Bank
Glasgow, MT
(406) 228-8231
www.fcbank.net

First State Bank
Thompson Falls, MT
(406) 827-3565
www.fsbtf.com

Flint Creek Valley Bank
Philipsburg, MT
(406) 859-3241

Independence Bank Havre, MT
(800) 823-2274
www.ibyourbank.com

Lake County Bank
Saint Ignatius, MT
(406) 745-3123

Montana First National Bank
Kalispell, MT
(406) 755-9999
www.ftibmontana.com

Valley Bank of Kalispell
Kalispell, MT
(406) 752-7123
www.valleybankmt.com

NEBRASKA

Beatrice National Bank &
Trust Co.
Beatrice, NE
(402) 223-3114
www.snb-beatrice.com

Centennial Bank
Omaha, NE
(402) 891-0003

City State Bank

Sutton, NE
(402) 773-5521

Commercial State Bank
Wausa, NE
(402) 586-2266
www.wausabank.com

Community Bank
Alma, NE
(308) 928-2929

Dakota County State Bank
South Sioux City, NE
(402) 494-4215
www.dcsb.com

Farmers & Merchants Bank
Milford, NE
(402) 761-7600
www.bankfmb.com

Farmers & Merchants State
Bank
Wayne, NE
(402) 375-2043
www.fandmstatebank.com

Farmers State Bank
Bennet, NE
(402) 782-3500

First National Bank in Ord
Ord, NE
(308) 728-3201

Gothenburg State Bank &
Trust Co.
Gothenburg, NE
 (308) 537-7181

Heritage Bank
Wood River, NE
 (308) 583-2262
www.bankonheritage.com

Midwest Bank
Pierce, NE
(402) 329-6221
www.midwestbanks.com

Saline State Bank
Wilber, NE
(402) 821-2241
www.salinestatebank.com

NEW JERSEY

1st Constitution Bank
Cranbury; NJ
(609) 655-4500
www.Istconstitution.com

Commerce Bank Shore
Forked River, NJ
(609) 693-1111
www.commerceonline.com

Interchange Bank
Saddle Brook, NJ
(201) 703-2265

www.interchangebank.com

Lakeland Bank
Newfoundland, NJ
(973) 697-2040
www.msnb.com

Panasia Bank
Fort Lee, NJ
(201) 947-6666
www.panasiabank.com

Skylands Community Bank
Hackettstown, NJ
 (908) 850-9010
www.skylandscombank.com

Woodstown National Bank
Woodstown, NJ
(856) 769-3300
www.woodstownbank.com

NEVADA

BankWest of Nevada
Las Vegas, NV
(702) 248-4200
www.bankwestofnevada.com

First National Bank
Ely, NV
(775) 289-4441

Heritage Bank of Nevada
Reno, NV

(775) 348-1000
www.heritagebanknevada.com

NEW HAMPSHIRE

Village Bank & Trust
Company
Gilford, NH
(603) 528-3000
www.villagebanknh.com

NEW MEXICO

Ambank
Silver City, NM
(505) 534-0550

Bank of the Rio Grande
National
Las Cruces, NM
(505) 525-8900
www.bank-riogrande.com

Citizens Bank of Clovis
Clovis, NM
(505) 769-1911
www.citizensbankofclovis.com

First National Bank of Las
Vegas Las Vegas, NM
(505) 425-7584

Valley Bank of Commerce
Roswell, NM
(505) 623-2265

NEW YORK

Adirondack Bank
Saranac Lake, NY
(518) 891-2323
www.adirondackbank.com

Bank of Castile
Castile, NY
(585) 493-2576
www.bankofcastile.com

Bath National Bank
Bath, NY
(607) 776-3381
www.bathnational.com

Capital Bank & Trust Co.
Albany, NY
(518) 434-1212
www.capitalbank.com

Cattaraugus County Bank
Little Valley, NY
(716) 938-9128
www.ccblv.com

Citibank
New York, NY
(800) 836-1324
www.citibank.com

Community Bank National
Canton, NY
(315) 386-8319
www.communitybankna.com

154

Ellenville National Bank
Ellenville, NY
(845) 647-4300
www.enbebank.com

First National Bank of Groton
Groton, NY
(607) 898-5871

National Bank of Coxsackie
Coxsackie, NY
(518) 731-6161
www.nbcoxsackie.com

National Bank of Geneva
Geneva, NY
(315) 789-2300
www.nbgeneva.com

Solvay Bank
Solvay, NY
(3 15) 468-1661
www.solvaybank.com

Suffolk County National Bank
Riverhead, NY
(631) 727-4712
www.scnb.com

Wyoming County Bank
(formerly Pavilion State Bank)
Pavilion, NY
(585) 584-3151
www.wycobank.com

NORTH CAROLINA

American Community Bank
Monroe, NC
(704) 225-8444

Catawba Valley Bank
Hickory, NC
(828) 431-2300
www.catawbavalleybank.com

Four Oaks Bank & Trust
Company
Four Oaks, NC
(919) 963-2177
www.fouroaksbank.com

Lumbee Guaranty Bank
Pembroke, NC
(910) 521-9707

Northwestern National Bank
Wilkesboro, NC
(336) 903-0600

Surrey Bank & Trust
Mount Airy NC
(336) 719-2310

Yadkin Valley Bank & Trust
Company
Elkin, NC
(336) 526-6301
www.yadkinvalleybank.com

NORTH DAKOTA

American State Bank and Trust
Co.
Williston, ND
(701) 774-4104
www.asbt.com

Community National Bank of
Grand Forks
Grand Forks, ND
(701) 780-7700
www.cnbgf.com

Dacotah Bank Valley City
Valley City ND
(701) 845-2712
www.dacotahbank.com

First United Bank
Park River, ND
(701) 284-7810
www.firstunitedonline.com

Security State Bank
Dunseith, ND
(701) 244-5795
www.securitystatebanknd.com

State Bank of Bottineau
Bottineau, ND
 (701) 228-2204
www.statebankofbottineau.com

First National Bank

Shelby, OH
(419) 342-4010
www.shelbyfnb.com

Stutsman County State Bank
Jamestown, ND
(701) 253-5600

Hicksville Bank
wwstutsmanbank.com
Hicksville, OH
(419) 542-7726
www.thehicksvillebank.com

United Community
Bank of North Dakota
Leeds, ND
(701) 466-2232
www.ucbnd.com

North Valley Bank
Zanesville, OH
(740) 450-2265
www.nvboh.com

United Valley Bank
Cavalier, ND
(701) 780-9757
www.uvbnd.com

Ohio Heritage Bank
Coshocton, OH
(740) 622-8311
www.ohioheritage.com

U.S. Bank

Fargo, ND
(701) 280-3500
www.usbank.com

Richwood Banking Co.
Richwood, OH
(740) 943-2317
www.richwoodbank.com

OHIO

Savings Bank
Circleville, OH
(740) 474-3191

1st National Community
BankEast Liverpool, OH
 (330) 385-9200
www.lstncb.com

Sutton Bank
Attica, OH
(419) 426-3641
www.suttonbank.com

Citizens Bank Co.
Beverly, OH
(740) 984-2381
www.thecitizens.com

Union Bank Co.
Columbus Grove, OH
(419) 659-2141
www.theubank.com

Farmers & Merchants Bank
Caldwell, OH
(740) 732-5621
www.farmersmerchants-bank.com

Vinton County National Bank
McArthur, OH
(740) 596-2525
www.vintoncomitybank.com

Wayne County National Bank
Wooster, OH
(330) 264-1222
www.wcnbwooster.com

OKLAHOMA

Bank of Cherokee County
Hulbert, OK
(918) 772-2572

Bank of Union Union City,
OK (405) 483-5308

Chickasha Bank & Trust
Company
Chickasha, OK
(405) 222-0550
www.chickashabank.com

Community State Bank
Poteau, OK
(918) 647-8101

First American Bank
Purcell, OK

(800) 522-1262
www.bankfab.com

First National Bank & Trust
Co.
Weatherford, OK
(580) 772-5574
www.fnbwford.com

First National Bank & Trust
Company
Chickasha, OK
(405) 224-2200
www.fnbchickasha.com

Firstbank
Antlers, OK
(580) 298-3368
www.firstbank-ok.com

Landmark Bank
Ada, OK
(580) 436-1117
www.landmarkbanks.com

Pauls Valley National Bank
Pauls Valley, OK
(405) 238-9321
www.pvnational.com

People's National Bank of
Checotah
Checotah, OK
(918) 473-2296

Security First National Bank of
Hugo
Hugo, OK
(580) 326-9641

OREGON

Columbia River Bank
The Dalles, OR
(877) 272-3678
www.columbiariverbank.com

Community Bank
Joseph, OR
(800) 472-4292
www.communitybanknet.com

Umpqua Bank
Roseburg, OR
www.umpquabank.com

PENNSYLVANIA
Community Bank & Trust
Company Clarks
Summit, PA
(570) 586-6876
www.combk.com

Community Banks
Millersburg, PA
(717) 692-4781
www.communitybanks.com

County National Bank
Clearfield, PA
(800) 492-3221

www.bankcnb.com

CSB Bank
Curwensville, PA
(800) 494-3453
www.csb-bank.com

First National Community
Bank
Dunmore, PA
(570) 348-4817
www.fncb.com

Hamlin Bank & Trust
Company
Smethport, PA
(814) 887-5555

Honesdale National Bank
Honesdale, PA
(570) 253-3355
www.hnbbank.com

Jersey Shore State Bank
Jersey Shore, PA
(570) 398-2213
wwjssb.com

Mercer County State Bank
Sandy Lake, PA
(724) 376-7015
www.mcsbank.com

New Tripoli National Bank
New Tripoli, PA

(610) 298-8811
www.ntnb.net

Old Forge Bank
Old Forge, PA
(570) 457-8345
www.oldforgebankpa.com

S & T Bank (formerly PFC
Bank)
Ford City, PA
(724) 763-1221
www.stbank.com

Union National Bank
Mount Cannel, PA
(570) 339-1040
www.unbmountcarmel.com

RHODE ISLAND

Washington Trust Co.
Westerly, RI
(401) 351-6240
www.washtrust.com

SOUTH CAROLINA

Anderson Bros. Bank
Mullins, SC
 (843) 464-6271

Bank of York
York, SC
(803) 684-2265

www.bankofyork.com

Community First Bank
Walhalla, SC
(864) 638-2105

Conway National Bank
Conway, SC
(843) 248-5721
www.conwaynationalbank.com

Enterprise Bank of South
Carolina
Ehrhardt, SC
(803) 267-4351
www.ebanksc.com

Hony County State Bank
Loris, SC
(843) 756-6333
www.horrycountystatebank.com

Palmetto State Bank
Hampton, SC
(803) 943-2671
www.palmettostatebank.com

SOUTH DAKOTA

Farmers & Merchants State
Bank
Iroquois, SD
(605) 546-2544

First Fidelity Bank
Burke, SD

(605) 775-2641
www.ffb-sd.com

First State Bank of Roscoe
Roscoe, SD
(605) 287-4451

First State Bank of Warner
Warner, SD
(605) 225-9605

Fulton State Bank
Fulton, SD
(605) 996-5731

Great Plains Bank
Eureka, SD
(605) 284-2633

Peoples State Bank
Summit, SD
(605) 398-6111

Peoples State Bank
De Smet, SD
(605) 854-3321

Merchants State Bank
Freeman, SD
(605) 925-4222
www.msb-sd.com

TENNESSEE

American City Bank
Tullahoma, TN

(931) 455-0026
www.americancitybank.com

Bank of Crockett
Bells, TN
(731) 663-2031
www.bankofcrockett.com

Citizens Bank
Carthage, TN
(615) 256-2912
www.citizens-bank.net

Citizens Bank of East
Tennessee
Rogersville, TN
(423) 272-2200

Citizens Community Bank
Winchester, TN
(931) 967-3342
www.ccbank.net

Commercial Bank & Trust Co.
Paris, TN
(73 1) 642-3341
www.cbtcnet.com

First Bank of Tennessee
Spring City, TN
(423) 365-8400
www.firstbanktn.com

First National Bank
Pikeville, TN

(423) 447-2931

First National Bank of
Manchester
Manchester, TN
(931) 728-3518
www.fnbmanchester.com

First Trust & Savings Bank
Oneida, TN
(423) 569-6313
www.ftsbonline.com

Macon Bank & Trust Co.
Lafayette, TN
(615) 666-2121
www.maconbankandtrust.com

Peoples Bank
Clifton, TN
(931) 676-3311
www.pbbanking.com

Peoples Bank & Trust Co. of
Pickett County
Byrdstown, TN
(931) 864-3168
www.peoplesbankbyrdstown.com

Traders National Bank
Tullahoma, TN
(931) 455-3426
www.tradersbank.com

TEXAS

161

City National Bank
Sulphur Springs, TX
(903) 885-7523
www.bank@cnb.com

First National Bank
Hughes Springs, TX
 (903) 639-2521
First National Bank
Newton, TX
(409) 379-8587

First National Bank
Borger, TX
(806) 273-2865
www.fnbborger.com

First National Bank
George West, TX
(361) 449-1571
www.fnbgw.com

First National Bank of Albany
Breckenridge
Albany, TX
(915) 762-2221

Peoples National Bank
Paris, TX
(903) 785-1099
www.pnbparis.com

Peoples State Bank
Clyde, TX
(325) 893-4211

Round Top State Bank
Round Top, TX
(979) 249-3151
 www.roundtopstatebank.com

Security Bank
Rails, TX
(806) 253-2511
www.security-bank.com

UTAH

Bonneville Bank
Provo, UT
(801) 374-9500
www.bonnevillebank.com

Transportation Alliance Bank
Ogden, UT
(801) 624-4800
www.tabbank.com

Village Bank
St. George, UT
(435) 674-5200
www.thevillagebank.com

Volvo Commercial Credit
Corp.
Utah Salt Lake City, UT
(801) 266-8522
www.acceltrans.com

Wright Express Financial
Services Corp.
Salt Lake City, UT

(801) 270-8166
www.wrightexpress.com

VERMONT

Peoples Trust Company of St.
Albans
St. Albans, VT
(802) 524-3773

VIRGINIA

Bank of Charlotte County
Phenix, VA
(434) 542-5111
www.bankofcharlotte.com

Bank of Hampton Roads
Chesapeake, VA
(757) 488-8700
www.bankofhamptonroads.com

Bank of Marion
Marion, VA
(276) 783-3116
www.bankofmarionva.com

Bank of Northumberland
Heathsville, VA
(804) 529-6158
www.bankofnorthumberland.net

Benchmark Community Bank
Kenbridge, VA
(434) 676-8444
www.bcbonline.com

Farmers & Miners Bank
Pennington Gap, VA
(276) 546-4692

Grayson National Bank
Independence, VA
(276) 773-2811

Highlands Union Bank
Abingdon, VA
(276) 628-9181
www.hubank.com

New Peoples Bank
Honaker, VA
(276) 873-6288
www.newpeoplesbank.com

Peoples Community Bank
Montross, VA
(360) 258-6329

Powell Valley National Bank
Jonesville, VA
(276) 346-1414
www.powellvalleybank.com

WASHINGTON

Americanwest Bank
Spokane, WA
(509) 467-9084
www.awbank.net

Bank of the Pacific
Aberdeen, WA
(888) 366-3267
www.thebankofpacific.com

Community First Bank
Kennewick, WA
(509) 783-3435
www.communitylst.com

First Heritage Bank
Snohomish, WA
(360) 568-0536
www.firstheritage.net

Islanders Bank
Friday Harbor, WA
 (360) 378-2265
www.islanders-bank.com

Mount Rainier National Bank
Enumclaw, WA
(360) 825-0100
www.mrnbank.com

Riverview Community Bank
(formerly Today's Bank)
Vancouver, WA
(804) 493-8031
www.riverviewbank.com

Security State Bank
Centralia, WA
(360) 736-2861
www.ssbwa.com

Whidbey Island Bank
Oak Harbor, WA
(360) 675-5968
www.wibank.com

WEST VIRGINIA

Bank of Gassaway
Gassaway, WV
(304) 364-5138

Bank of Romney
Romney, WV
(304) 822-3541
www.bankofromney.net

Calhoun City Bank
Grantsville, WV
(304) 354-6116
www.calhounbanks.com

Community Bank of
Parkersburg
Parkersburg, WV
(304) 485-7991
www.communitybankpkbg.com

Pendleton County Bank
Franklin, WV
(304) 358-2311
www.yourbank.com

Poca Valley Bank
Walton, WV
(304) 577-6611
 www.pocavalleybank.com

Traders Bank
Spencer, WV
(304) 927-3340
www.tradersbanking.com

WISCONSIN

Chippewa Valley Bank
Winter, WI
(715) 266-3501
www.chippewavalleybank.com

Community Bank
Superior, WI
(715) 392-8241
www.communitybanksuperior.com

Community Bank of Central
Wisconsin
Colby, WI
(715) 223-3998
www.conrnbnk.com

Community Bank of Oconto
County
Oconto Falls, WI
(920) 846-2810
www.communitybankoc.com

First National Bank Manitowoc
Manitowoc, WI
(920) 684-6611
www.bankfirstnational.com

Fortress Bank of Westby

Westby, WI
(608) 634-3787
wwrw.fortressbanks.com

Laona State Bank
Laona, WI
(715) 674-2911

Northern State Bank
Ashland, WI
(7 15) 682-2772
www.nsbashland.com

Premier Community Bank
Marion, WI
(715) 754-2535
www.premiercommunity.com

Reedsburg Bank
Reedsburg, WI
(608) 524-8251
www.reedsburgbank.com

Royal Bank
Elroy, WI
(608) 462-8163
www.royalbank-usa.com

Shell Lake State Bank
Shell Lake, WI
(715) 468-7858
www.shelllakestatebank.com

WYOMING

165

Bank of Commerce
Rawlins, WY
(307) 324-2265
www.bocrawlins.com

Bank of Star Valley
Afton, WY
(307) 885-0000
www.bosv.com

Cowboy State Bank
Ranchester, WY
(307) 655-2291

First National Bank & Trust
Co.
Powell, WY
(307) 754-2201
www.powellbank.com

First National Bank of Buffalo
Buffalo, WY
(307) 684-2555
www.fnb-buffalo.com

First State Bank of
Wheatland
Wheatland, WY
(307) 322-5222
www.fsbwy.com

Hilltop National Bank
Casper, WY
 (307) 265-2740
www.hnbwyo.com

MIKE ENEMIGO PRESENTS

THE CELL BLOCK

MIKE ENEMIGO is the new prison/street art sensation who has written and published several books. He is inspired by emotion; hope; pain; dreams and nightmares. He physically lives somewhere in a California prison cell where he works relentlessly creating his next piece. His mind and soul are elsewhere; seeing, studying, learning, and drawing inspiration to tear down suppressive walls and inspire the culture by pushing artistic boundaries.

THE CELL BLOCK is an independent multimedia company with the objective of accurately conveying the prison/street experience with the credibility and honesty that only one who has lived it can deliver, through literature and other arts, and to entertain and enlighten while doing so. Everything published by The Cell Block has been created by a prisoner, while in a prison cell.

THE BEST RESOURCE DIRECTORY FOR PRISONERS, $17.95 & $5.00 S/H: This book has over 1,450 resources for prisoners! Includes: Pen-Pal Companies! Non-Nude Photo Sellers! Free Books and Other Publications! Legal Assistance! Prisoner Advocates! Prisoner Assistants! Correspondence Education! Money-Making Opportunities! Resources for Prison Writers, Poets, Artists! And much, much more! Anything you can think of doing from your prison cell, this book contains the resources to do it!

A GUIDE TO RELAPSE PREVENTION FOR PRISONERS, $15.00 & $5.00 S/H: This book provides the information and guidance that can make a real difference in the preparation of a comprehensive relapse prevention plan. Discover how to meet the parole board's expectation using these proven and practical principles. Included is a blank template and sample relapse prevention plan to assist in your preparation.

THEE ENEMY OF THE STATE (SPECIAL EDITION), $9.99 & $4.00 S/H: Experience the inspirational journey of a kid who was introduced to the art of rapping in 1993, struggled between his dream of becoming a professional rapper and the reality of the streets, and was finally offered a recording deal in 1999, only to be arrested minutes later and eventually sentenced to life in prison for murder... However, despite his harsh reality, he dedicated himself to hip-hop once again, and with resilience and determination, he sets out to prove he may just be one of the dopest rhyme writers/spitters ever .... At this point, it becomes deeper than rap .... Welcome to a preview of the greatest story you never heard.

LOST ANGELS: $15.00 & $5.00: David Rodrigo was a child who belonged to no world; rejected for his mixed heritage by most of his family and raised by an outcast uncle in the mean streets of East L.A. Chance cast him into a far darker and more devious pit of intrigue that stretched from the barest gutters to the halls of power in the great city. Now, to survive the clash of lethal forces arrayed about him, and to protect those he loves, he has only two allies; his quick wits, and the flashing blade that earned young David the street name, Viper.

LOYALTY AND BETRAYAL DELUXE EDITION, $19.99 & $7.00 S/H: Chunky was an associate of and soldier for the notorious Mexican Mafia – La Eme. That is, of course, until he was betrayed by those, he was most loyal to. Then he vowed to become their worst enemy. And though they've attempted to kill him numerous times, he still to this day is running around making a mockery of their organization .... This is the story of how it all began.

MONEY IZ THE MOTIVE: SPECIAL 2-IN-1 EDITION, $19.99 & $7.00 S/H: Like most kids growing up in the hood, Kano has a dream of going from rags to riches. But when his plan to get fast money by robbing the local "mom and pop" shop goes wrong, he quickly finds himself sentenced to serious prison time. Follow Kano as he is schooled to the ways of the game by some of the most respected OGs whoever did it; then is set free and given the resources to put his schooling into action and build the ultimate hood empire...

DEVILS & DEMONS: PART 1, $15.00 & $5.00 S/H: When Talton leaves the West Coast to set up shop in Florida he meets the female version of himself: A drug dealing murderess with psychological issues. A whirlwind of sex, money and murder inevitably ensues and Talton finds himself on the run from the law with nowhere to turn to. When his team from home finds out he's in trouble, they get on a plane heading south...

DEVILS & DEMONS: PART 2, $15.00 & $5.00 S/H: The Game is bitter-sweet for Talton, aka Gangsta. The same West Coast Clique who came to his aid ended up putting bullets into the chest of the woman he had fallen in love with. After leaving his ride or die in a puddle of her own blood, Talton finds himself on a flight back to Oak Park, the neighborhood where it all started...

DEVILS & DEMONS: PART 3, $15.00 & $5.00 S/H: Talton is on the road to retribution for the murder of the love of his life. Dante and his crew of killers are on a path of no return. This urban classic is based on real-life West Coast underworld politics. See what happens when a group of YG's find themselves in the midst of real underworld demons...

DEVILS & DEMONS: PART 4, $15.00 & $5.00 S/H: After waking up from a coma, Alize has locked herself away from the rest of the world. When her sister Brittany and their friend finally take her on a girl's night out, she meets Luck – a drug dealing womanizer.

FREAKY TALES, $15.00 & $5.00 S/H: Freaky Tales is the first book in a brand-new erotic series. King Guru, author of the *Devils & Demons* books, has put together a collection of sexy short stories and memoirs. In true TCB fashion, all of the erotic tales included in this book have been loosely based on true accounts told to, or experienced by the author.

THE ART & POWER OF LETTER WRITING FOR PRISONERS: DELUXE EDITION $19.99 & $7.00 S/H: When locked inside a prison cell, being able to write well is the most powerful skill you can have! Learn how to increase your power by writing high-quality personal and formal letters! Includes letter templates, pen-pal website strategies, punctuation guide and more!

THE PRISON MANUAL: $24.99 & $7.00 S/H: *The Prison Manual* is your all-in-one book on how to not only survive the rough terrain of the American prison system, but use it to your advantage so you can THRIVE from it! How to Use Your Prison Time to YOUR Advantage; How to Write Letters that Will Give You Maximum Effectiveness; Workout and Physical Health Secrets that Will Keep You as FIT as Possible; The Psychological impact of incarceration and How to Maintain Your MAXIMUM Level of Mental Health; Prison Art Techniques; Fulfilling Food Recipes; Parole Preparation Strategies and much, MUCH more!

GET OUT, STAY OUT!, $16.95 & $5.00 S/H: This book should be in the hands of everyone in a prison cell. It reveals a challenging but clear course for overcoming the obstacles that stand between prisoners and their freedom. For those behind bars, one goal outshines all others: GETTING OUT! After being released, that goal then shifts to STAYING OUT! This book will help prisoners do both. It has been masterfully constructed into five parts that will help prisoners maximize focus while they strive to accomplish whichever goal is at hand.

MOB$TAR MONEY, $12.00 & $4.00 S/H: After Trey's mother is sent to prison for 75 years to life, he and his little brother are moved from their home in Sacramento, California, to his grandmother's house in Stockton, California where he is forced to find his way in life and become a man on his own in the city's grimy streets. One day, on his way home from the local corner store, Trey has a rough encounter with the neighborhood bully. Luckily, that's when Tyson, a member of the MOBTAR, a local "get money" gang comes to his aid. The two kids quickly become friends, and it doesn't take long before Trey is embraced into the notorious MOB$TAR money gang, which opens the door to an adventure full of sex, money, murder and mayhem that will change his life forever... You will never guess how this story ends!

BLOCK MONEY, $12.00 & $4.00 S/H: Beast, a young thug from the grimy streets of central Stockton, California lives The

Block; breathes The Block; and has committed himself to bleed The Block for all it's worth until his very last breath. Then, one day, he meets Nadia; a stripper at the local club who piques his curiosity with her beauty, quick-witted intellect and rider qualities. The problem? She has a man – Esco – a local kingpin with money and power. It doesn't take long, however, before a devious plot is hatched to pull off a heist worth an indeterminable amount of money. Following the acts of treachery, deception and betrayal are twists and turns and a bloody war that will leave you speechless!

HOW TO HUSTLE AND WIN: SEX, MONEY, MURDER EDITION $15.00 & $5.00 S/H: *How To Hu$tle and Win: Sex, Money, Murder Edition* is the grittiest, underground self-help manual for the 21st century street entrepreneur in print. Never has there been such a book written for today's gangsters, goons and go-getters. This self-help handbook is an absolute must-have for anyone who is actively connected to the streets.

RAW LAW: YOUR RIGHTS, & HOW TO SUE WHEN THEY ARE VIOLATED! $15.00 & $5.00 S/H: *Raw Law For Prisoners* is a clear and concise guide for prisoners and their advocates to understanding civil rights laws guaranteed to prisoners under the US Constitution, and how to successfully file a lawsuit when those rights have been violated! From initial complaint to trial, this book will take you through the entire process, step by step, in simple, easy-to-understand terms. Also included are several examples where prisoners have sued prison officials successfully, resulting in changes of unjust rules and regulations and recourse for rights violations, oftentimes resulting in rewards of thousands, even millions of dollars in damages! If you feel your rights have been violated, don't lash out at guards, which is usually ineffective and only makes matters worse. Instead, defend yourself successfully by using the legal system, and getting the power of the courts on your side!

HOW TO WRITE URBAN BOOKS FOR MONEY & FAME: $16.95 & $5.00 S/H: Inside this book you will learn the true story of how Mike Enemigo and King Guru have received money and fame from inside their prison cells by writing urban books; the secrets to writing hood classics so you, too, can be caked up and famous; proper punctuation using hood examples; and resources you can use to achieve your money motivated ambitions! If you're a prisoner who want to write urban novels for money and fame, this must-have manual will give you all the game!

PRETTY GIRLS LOVE BAD BOYS: AN INMATE'S GUIDE TO GETTING GIRLS: $15.00 & $5.00 S/H: Tired of the same, boring, cliché pen pal books that don't tell you what you really need to know? If so, this book is for you! Anything you need to know on the art of long and short distance seduction is included within these pages! Not only does it give you the science of attracting pen pals from websites, it also includes psychological profiles and instructions on how to seduce any woman you set your sights on! Includes interviews of women who have fallen in love with prisoners, bios for pen pal ads, pre-written love letters, romantic poems, love-song lyrics, jokes and much, much more! This book is the ultimate guide – a must-have for any prisoner who refuses to let prison walls affect their MAC'n.

THE LADIES WHO LOVE PRISONERS, $15.00 & $5.00 S/H: New Special Report reveals the secrets of real women who have fallen in love with prisoners, regardless of crime, sentence, or location. This info will give you a HUGE advantage in getting girls from prison.

THE MILLIONAIRE PRISONER: PART 1, $16.95 & $5.00 S/H

THE MILLIONAIRE PRISONER: PART 2, $16.95 & $5.00 S/H

THE MILLIONAIRE PRISONER: SPECIAL 2-IN-1 EDITION, $24.99 & $7.00 S/H: Why wait until you get out of prison to achieve your dreams? Here's a blueprint that you can use to become successful! *The Millionaire Prisoner* is your complete reference to overcoming any obstacle in prison. You won't be able to put it down! With this book you will discover the secrets to: Making money from your cell! Obtain FREE money for correspondence courses! Become an expert on any topic! Develop the habits of the rich! Network with celebrities! Set up your own website! Market your products, ideas and services! Successfully

172

use prison pen pal websites! All of this and much, much more! This book has enabled thousands of prisoners to succeed and it will show you the way also!

THE MILLIONAIRE PRISONER 3: SUCCESS UNIVERSITY, $16.95 & $5 S/H: Why wait until you get out of prison to achieve your dreams? Here's a new-look blueprint that you can use to be successful! *The Millionaire Prisoner 3* contains advanced strategies to overcoming any obstacle in prison. You won't be able to put it down!

THE MILLIONAIRE PRISONER 4: PEN PAL MASTERY, $16.95 & $5.00 S/H: Tired of subpar results? Here's a master blueprint that you can use to get tons of pen pals! *TMP 4: Pen Pal Mastery* is your complete roadmap to finding your one true love. You won't be able to put it down! With this book you'll DISCOVER the SECRETS to: Get FREE pen pals & which sites are best to use; Successful tactics female prisoners can win with; Use astrology to find love; friendship & more; Build a winning social media presence; Playing phone tag & successful sex talk; Hidden benefits of foreign pen pals; Find your success mentors; Turning "hits" into friendships; Learn how to write letters/emails that get results. All of this and much more!

GET OUT, GET RICH: HOW TO GET PAID LEGALLY WHEN YOU GET OUT OF PRISON!, $16.95 & $5.00 S/H: Many of you are incarcerated for a money-motivated crime. But w/ today's tech & opportunities, not only is the crime-for-money risk/reward ratio not strategically wise, it's not even necessary. You can earn much more money by partaking in any one of the easy, legal hustles explained in this book, regardless of your record. Help yourself earn an honest income so you can not only make a lot of money, but say good-bye to penitentiary chances and prison forever! (Note: Many things in this book can even he done from inside prison.) (ALSO PUBLISHED AS *HOOD MILLIONAIRE: HOW TO HUSTLE AND WIN LEGALLY!*)

THE CEO MANUAL: HOW TO START A BUSINESS WHEN YOU GET OUT OF PRISON, $16.95 & $5.00 S/H: $16.95 & $5 S/H: This new book will teach you the simplest way to start your own business when you get out of prison. Includes:

Start-up Steps! The Secrets to Pulling Money from Investors! How to Manage People Effectively! How To Legally Protect Your Assets from "them"! Hundreds of resources to get you started, including a list of "loan friendly" banks! (ALSO PUBLISHED AS *CEO MANUAL: START A BUSINESS, BE A BOSS!*)

THE MONEY MANUAL: UNDERGROUND CASH SECRETS EXPOSED! 16.95 & $5.00 S/H: Becoming a millionaire is equal parts what you make, and what you don't spend – AKA save. All Millionaires and Billionaires have mastered the art of not only making money, but keeping the money they make (remember Donald Trump's tax maneuvers?), as well as establishing credit so that they are loaned money by banks and trusted with money from investors: AKA OPM – other people's money. And did you know there are millionaires and billionaires just waiting to GIVE money away? It's true! These are all very-little known secrets "they" don't want YOU to know about, but that I'm exposing in my new book!

HOOD MILLIONAIRE; HOW TO HUSTLE & WIN LEGALLY, $16.95 & $5.00 S/H: Hustlin' is a way of life in the hood. We all have money motivated ambitions, not only because we gotta eat, but because status is oftentimes determined by one's own salary. To achieve what we consider financial success, we often invest our efforts into illicit activities – we take penitentiary chances. This leads to a life in and out of prison, sometimes death – both of which are counterproductive to gettin' money. But there's a solution to this, and I have it...

CEO MANUAL: START A BUSINESS BE A BOSS, $16.95 & $5.00 S/H: After the success of the urban-entrepreneur classic *Hood Millionaire: How To Hustle & Win Legally!*, self-made millionaires Mike Enemigo and Sav Hustle team back up to bring you the latest edition of the Hood Millionaire series – *CEO Manual: Start A Business, Be A Boss!* In this latest collection of game laying down the art of "hoodpreneurship", you will learn such things as: 5 Core Steps to Starting Your Own Business! 5 Common Launch Errors You Must Avoid! How To Write a Business Plan! How To Legally Protect Your Assets From "Them"! How To Make Your Business Fundable, Where to Get

Money for Your Start-up Business, and even How to Start a Business With No Money! You will learn How to Drive Customers to Your Website, How to Maximize Marketing Dollars, Contract Secrets for the savvy boss, and much, much more! And as an added bonus, we have included over 200 Business Resources, from government agencies and small business development centers, to a secret list of small-business friendly banks that will help you get started!

PAID IN FULL: WELCOME TO DA GAME, $15.00 & $5.00 S/H. In 1983, the movie *Scarface* inspired many kids growing up in America's inner cities to turn their rags into riches by becoming cocaine kingpins. Harlem's Azie Faison was one of them. Faison would ultimately connect with Harlem's Rich Porter and Alpo Martinez, and the trio would go on to become certified street legends of the '80s and early '90s. Years later, Dame Dash and Roc-A-Fella Films would tell their story in the based-on-actual-events movie, *Paid in Full*. But now, we are telling the story our way – The Cell Block way – where you will get a perspective of the story that the movie did not show, ultimately learning an outcome that you did not expect. Book one of our series, *Paid in Full: Welcome to da Game*, will give you an inside look at a key player in this story, one that is not often talked about – Lulu, the Columbian cocaine kingpin with direct ties to Pablo Escobar, who plugged Azie in with an unlimited amount of top-tier cocaine at dirt-cheap prices that helped boost the trio to neighborhood superstars and certified kingpin status... until greed, betrayal, and murder destroyed everything....

OJ'S LIFE BEHIND BARS, $15.00 & $5 S/H: In 1994, Heisman Trophy winner and NFL superstar OJ Simpson was arrested for the brutal murder of his ex-wife Nicole Brown-Simpson and her friend Ron Goldman. In 1995, after the "trial of the century," he was acquitted of both murders, though most of the world believes he did it. In 2007 OJ was again arrested, but this time in Las Vegas, for armed robbery and kidnapping. On October 3, 2008 he was found guilty sentenced to 33 years and was sent to Lovelock Correctional Facility, in Lovelock, Nevada. There he met inmate-author Vernon Nelson. Vernon was granted a true, insider's perspective into the mind and life of one of the country's most notorious men; one that has never been provided…until now.

BLINDED BY BETRAYAL, $15.00 & $5.00 S/H. Khalil wanted nothing more than to chase his rap dream when he got out of prison. After all, a fellow inmate had connected him with a major record producer that could help him take his career to unimaginable heights, and his girl is in full support of his desire to trade in his gun for a mic. Problem is, Khalil's crew, the notorious Blood Money Squad, awaited him with open arms, unaware of his desire to leave the game alone, and expected him to jump head first into the life of fast money and murder. Will Khalil be able to balance his desire to get out of the game with the expectations of his gang to participate in it? Will he be able to pull away before it's too late? Or, will the streets pull him right back in, ultimately causing his demise? One thing for sure, the streets are loyal to no one, and blood money comes with bloody consequences....

THE MOB, $16.99 & $5 S/H. PaperBoy is a Bay Area boss who has invested blood, sweat, and years into building *The Mob* – a network of Bay Area Street legends, block bleeders, and underground rappers who collaborate nationwide in the interest of pushing a multi-million-dollar criminal enterprise of sex, drugs, and murder.

AOB, $15.00 & $5 S/H. Growing up in the Bay Area, Manny Fresh the Best had a front-row seat to some of the coldest players to ever do it. And you already know, A.O.B. is the name of the Game! So, When Manny Fresh slides through Stockton one day and sees Rosa, a stupid-bad Mexican chick with a whole lotta 'talent' behind her walking down the street tryna get some money, he knew immediately what he had to do: Put it In My Pocket!

AOB 2, $15.00 & $5 S/H.

AOB 3, $15.00 & $5 S/H

PIMPOLOGY: THE 7 ISMS OF THE GAME, $15.00 & $5 S/H: It's been said that if you knew better, you'd do better. So, in the spirit of dropping jewels upon the rare few who truly want to know how to win, this collection of exclusive Game has been compiled. And though a lot of so-called players claim to know how the Pimp Game is supposed to go, none have revealed the real. . . Until now!

JAILHOUSE PUBLISHING FOR MONEY, POWER & FAME: $24.99 & $7 S/H: In 2010, after flirting with the idea for two years, Mike Enemigo started writing his first book. In 2014, he officially launched his publishing company, The Cell Block, with the release of five books. Of course, with no mentor(s), how-to guides, or any real resources, he was met with failure after failure as he tried to navigate the treacherous goal of publishing books from his prison cell. However, he was determined to make it. He was determined to figure it out and he refused to quit. In Mike's new book, *Jailhouse Publishing for Money, Power, and Fame,* he breaks down all his jailhouse publishing secrets and strategies, so you can do all he's done, but without the trials and tribulations he's had to go through...

KITTY KAT, ADULT ENTERTAINMENT RESOURCE BOOK, $24.99 & $7.00 S/H: This book is jam packed with hundreds of sexy non nude photos including photo spreads. The book contains the complete info on sexy photo sellers, hot magazines, page turning bookstore, sections on strip clubs, porn stars, alluring models, thought provoking stories and must-see movies.

PRISON LEGAL GUIDE, $24.99 & $7.00 S/H: The laws of the U.S. Judicial system are complex, complicated, and always growing and changing. Many prisoners spend days on end digging through its intricacies. Pile on top of the legal code the rules and regulations of a correctional facility, and you can see how high the deck is being stacked against you. Correct legal information is the key to your survival when you have run afoul of the system (or it is running afoul of you). Whether you are an accomplished jailhouse lawyer helping newbies learn the ropes, an old head fighting bare-knuckle for your rights in the courts, or a hustler just looking to beat the latest write-up – this book has something for you!

PRISON HEALTH HANDBOOK, $19.99 & $7.00 S/H: *The Prison Health Handbook* is your one-stop go-to source for information on how to maintain your best health while inside the American prison system. Filled with information, tips, and secrets from doctors, gurus, and other experts, this book will educate you on such things as proper workout and exercise regimens; yoga benefits for prisoners; how to meditate effectively; pain management tips; sensible dieting solutions; nutritional knowledge; an understanding of various cancers, diabetes, hepatitis, and other diseases all too common in prison; how to effectively deal with mental health issues such as stress, PTSD, anxicty, and depression; a list of things your doctors DON'T want YOU to know; and much, much more!

All books are available on thecellblock.net.

You can also order by sending a money order or institutional check to:

The Cell Block
PO Box 1025
Rancho Cordova, CA 95741

Made in the USA
Monee, IL
13 November 2024